Ready to Minister

READY TO MINISTER

WILLIAM M. PINSON, JR.

BROADMAN PRESS
Nashville, Tennessee

Library of Congress Cataloging in Publication Data

Pinson, William M.
  Ready to minister.

  1. Pastoral theology.   I. Title.
BV4011.P52   1984   253   84-3052
ISBN 0-8054-3109-8

*This book is dedicated to
all Christian ministers
who have given themselves
in service to others.*

Preface

Why a book on ministry in a series on Christian leadership? Because the two go together. Leadership is a form of ministry, but more important, Christian leaders are to be servant-leaders, ministering to others. A Christian is not ready to lead until he is ready to minister.

As with the other volumes in the Broadman Leadership Series, this book is for all Christians who lead and minister but is especially suitable for those in church-related employment.

Basically this is a positive book, not majoring on the difficulties, pitfalls, or sacrifices of service. The following pages were written with a deep commitment to Christian ministry and a solid belief in the adventure of ministry. I have enjoyed my experiences in ministry, finding in them rich satisfaction. I pray these words will help others find the same joy and fulfillment.

Furthermore, this is primarily a nontechnical volume, not scholarly in the sense of numerous footnotes and lengthy bibliography. Essentially this book follows a biblical approach—based on what the Bible says about ministry—rather than a psychological, sociological, or theological approach. More than a quarter of a century as a Bible teacher and preacher has left me convinced that what we say ought to be rooted in the Scripture.

This volume is an introduction, an overview, a guide to further in-depth study. Subsequent volumes will flesh out the skeletal approach of this book. Matters only touched on here will be fully developed in following volumes of the Broadman Leadership Series.

Some matters are discussed in more than one chapter. The Bible, prayer, and faith, for example, relate to ministry in several ways and are dealt with from more than one perspective. The discussions on the Bible are a case in point. The Bible's content is a part of the bases for ministry; knowledge of the Bible is essential for ministry; interpreting the Bible is a skill needed for ministry; Bible study is a means of spiritual development which enhances ministry. As you read, keep in mind the context for the different approaches to similar subjects.

This book is the product of the labor of many persons. Doran McCarty assisted in the overall planning and editing. Doris Tinker, co-worker and secretary, helped type the preliminary drafts, typed the final copy, and guided the project to completion. Numerous persons read earlier drafts of the volume and made many helpful suggestions for improvement.

Our entire family was involved in the process of writing. Bobbie, beautiful wife and mother, helped to provide the setting which made writing possible. Our daughter Meredith helped type the first draft. Our daughter Allison contributed encouragement and understanding. Without the loving support of these three beautiful Christians, this volume could not have been written.

Numerous others made significant contributions—my professors from colleges and seminaries; co-workers in seminary, church, and denominational life; former students; friends in ministry; and authors who have penned insightful words on Christian ministry.

I have written these pages with the conviction that in the final analysis life ought to be evaluated not by how much we know about ministry or how much we have developed our ministry skills or how much we have matured in Christ, but by how effectively we have served others in Christ's name to the glory of God. Knowledge must be utilized and skills exercised to the benefit of those in need before we hear the Master say, "Well done, good, faithful servant."

WILLIAM M. PINSON, JR.
Dallas, Texas
June 1983

Contents

Ready to Minister

Introduction

The conference was over, and a number of us gathered for lunch before heading home. Around the table sat half a dozen effective Christian ministers—pastors, directors of education, denominational workers. The conversation turned to leadership and ministry. Why do some function well in ministry and others poorly? Is ministry a gift to be exercised or a skill to be developed? We talked on into the afternoon, never arriving at any final conclusions but agreeing that the development of effective ministers is a top priority.

A few days later an outstanding Christian businessman called to tell me that he and several other laymen were putting together a nationwide conference for lay leaders. He said they all considered themselves ministers with gifts to utilize in serving others. He emphasized that the world was never going to be won by the professionals—the pastors and missionaries—alone, but that all ministers needed to be involved. He asked me to speak at the conference on the subject of ministry as an opportunity and responsibility for all Christians.

These two incidents highlight the fact that the so-called "clergy" and "laity" agree on the importance of effective ministry and leadership. They realize that leadership and ministry are essential for carrying out the command of Christ to love the entire world and introduce everyone to God's saving power through faith in Christ. On every hand people are talking about the nature of ministry and leadership. That's what this book is about.

The Nature of Ministry

Ministry or service is the vocation of the Christian. Helping others in Christ's name to the glory of God is how we are to spend our days—

evangelizing, enabling, teaching, comforting, discipling, leading, encouraging, challenging, assisting. Ministry is the way to greatness in the Christian life. Jesus said, "Whosoever will be great among you, shall be your minister; And whosoever of you will be the chiefest, shall be servant of all. For even the Son of man came not to be ministered unto, but to minister, and to give his life a ransom for many" (Mark 10:43-45).

In a sense we Christians are all ministers. The call to salvation is a call to service (2 Tim. 1:9). The vocation we are challenged to "walk worthy of" is that of ministry in Christ's name (Eph. 4:1). Our activities and relationships should be viewed either as a means to or an opportunity for ministry.

Ministry is not necessarily something done at the church house. I banged head-on into this truth a few years ago when I met Sid Maples. I was preaching in a church in a medium-sized city in a typical morning worship service when the invitation exploded into what appeared to be something akin to an old-fashioned revival meeting. Any impression I might have had that my sermon was the cause was quickly shattered. As I greeted person after person coming down the aisle, each said, "Sid Maples shared with me." "Sid Maples ministered to me." "Sid Maples helped me."

Of course, you know what I did as soon as possible—I looked up Sid Maples. He was a small, unassuming, none-too-handsome man, a pawnbroker by trade. People who come into pawn shops to hock items are usually in crisis, trouble, or grief. He used his job to minister to persons in the midst of their brokenness. He shared Christ with them. He gave them love and concern. He helped them put life together again. He was an apostle in a pawn shop.

Since that time I have met thousands of Christians who minister in their daily routines. They believe that ministry is an opportunity for all. This book is, therefore, for all Christians who want to serve others in Christ's name. All God's family should be ministers. Unfortunately, *minister* is often thought of as a noun, as a title attached to someone in a "religious job." It is better understood as a verb related to the daily action of the Christian serving others. Thus every Christian ought to be able to say, "I minister."

Certain Christians are gifted with special ministry abilities. Paul, the great missionary apostle, wrote to the church in Ephesus, "Whereof I was made a minister, according to the gift of the grace of God given unto me by the effectual working of his power" (Eph. 3:7). Paul wrote to Timothy, "Neglect not the gift that is in thee, which was given thee by prophecy, with the laying on of the hands of the presbytery" (1 Tim. 4:14).

Other Christians are called to minister in certain positions, such as that of pastor, evangelist, deacon, or teacher. Paul spoke of himself as being "called to be an apostle" (Rom. 1:1) and indicated that God "gave some, apostles; and some, prophets; and some, evangelists; and some, pastors and teachers" (Eph. 4:11).

The Scriptures also reveal that some Christians receive a special calling to certain ministry tasks. Paul felt a very clear call to "preach among the Gentiles the unsearchable riches of Christ" (Eph. 3:8). He responded to what we would term a "call to missions."

Note that the special callings to minister—whether by gift or position or task—all relate to equipping the total family of God for ministry. Paul in his letter to the Ephesians indicated that special gifts were bestowed upon certain believers in order for them to be able to equip others to carry out the work of ministry (Eph. 4:7,11-16). So, although some have a special gifting or calling, all of God's people are to be ministers.

Preparing for Ministry

If ministry is a calling, something of a gift, how can a person get ready for it? Are we simply to receive it, or is there something we are to do in order to prepare for it? The Bible indicates that ministry is a gift or calling for all believers but that through preparation we may become available to God for certain special ministries (Gal. 1:15-18).

Although the calling to ministry is a gift from God—an act of God's grace—we are responsible for doing our best in the exercise of ministry. God not only expects us to exercise our gift of ministry but also to develop our ability to use it. We are to prepare ourselves for effective ministry.

Yet we cannot wait to begin to minister until we are completely ready to minister. We will never be perfectly prepared, and if we wait for that, we will never minister. Furthermore, we learn to minister while ministering. Thus only by plunging into the service of others will we become skilled servants. Ministry is a lifelong adventure—preparing to minister, ministering, and learning to minister more effectively. This book is a tool to help in each of those stages—in preparation, in ministry, and in learning to minister better. It is an introduction—really an overview—for those beginning to minister as well as a review for those already deep in the practice of ministry.

How do you know when you are ready to minister? When you are improving in ministry? When you are a success in ministry? These questions are difficult, if not impossible, to answer. Perhaps the best approach for the Christian minister is to find what God requires, be faithful to that, and trust God for the evaluation. Some may be surprised when they hear the Lord say, "Well done, good and faithful servant" (Matt. 25:21).

The Components of Ministry

What indeed does ministry involve? The best analogy I have seen to the components of effective ministry is a cable car or train. When we lived in the San Francisco Bay Area, I was continually intrigued by the cable cars and by BART, the Bay Area Rapid Transit system, trains powered by electricity. The ancient cable cars clanging up and down the hills hauling people here and there in good weather and bad were something of a symbol to me of service. So was the electric-powered train—the epitome of modernization—sleek, streamlined, computerized, dashing rapidly along ribbons of steel under the bay, through mountains, and beneath city streets, carrying thousands of persons daily. These two forms of transportation differed greatly in speed, size, modernness—but they were alike in the basics. Our service in Christ may differ in form, but the basics remain the same.

Both the cable car and the train ran on two rails resting on a solid base with power coming from an outside source. The elements of Christian ministry are similar. The *base* on which ministry rests is made up of a solid relation with God, one's self, and other persons. The *two rails* on which ministry moves forward are knowledge and skill. Both are essential. Knowledge is necessary for ministry (2 Pet. 1:5). We need to know some things in order to serve. Skills are also required for service. We need to be able to do some things in order to minister. Linked together, knowledge and skill help make ministry possible. Our source of *power* is God, and we must equip our lives to utilize that power efficiently.

This book is about these four elements of Christian ministry. Preparing for ministry involves all four of them. Ministry is how we are to spend our lives and is too important to take lightly. Ministry ought to be effective, not sloppy. And effective ministry calls for preparation and training. These pages intend to encourage that preparation and training as well as suggest how to obtain it. Now that we know where we are going and basically how we are going to try to get there, let's begin. My prayer is that *Ready to Minister* will indeed equip all who read it to become even more ready to minister.

PART I
Bases for Ministry

Most of my growing-up years were spent living by railroad tracks. When trains came through, the windows in our house would rattle and conversation would come to a stop because the noise was so loud we could not hear one another talking. Our family was accustomed to the trains and paid no attention to them, but overnight guests were sometimes frightened out of their wits by the roar in the night.

Trains had the same fascination for me as they do for most children— and adults, too, for that matter. I spent hours playing on the boxcars and walking the rails and crossties. I learned the art of balancing to run down a rail and the strategy of matching one's gait to the distance between the crossties.

I picked up many a rock from the roadbed without ever giving thought to how it got there or what it was for. Later as an adult who enjoyed riding trains, I became aware of the importance of the roadbed. While living in the northeastern part of the United States, I learned that the trains on which I rode adjusted their speed according to the condition of the bed. On some stretches we slowed to a crawl because the bed was in such poor condition that the ride would have been too rough at normal speed. The first massive train wreck I viewed was the result of a washed-out roadbed. Huge boxcars were strewed across the area like so many broken toys. Regardless of the condition of the engine and cars, if the roadbed is in poor shape the train will be slowed or derailed. A strong, stable, well-maintained bed is essential for a railroad.

Similarly, the base on which ministry rests is vitally important. Some persons, motivated either by guilt or a spurt of compassion, dash out to minister, only to fail. Why? Because ministry must rest on a solid foundation in order to be effective, and they lack that. What does this foundation involve?

The base on which ministry rests is similar in many ways to the roadbed for the train. It must have great strength, the strength that only God can provide. There must be stability, the stability of a responsible person being made whole through Jesus Christ and reaching out in love to others. There must be an awareness of needs and of the resources and approaches to meet those needs.

Thus, the bases for ministry involve our relation to God, to ourselves, and to others. Having a solid base for ministry is no guarantee that we will effectively help others. Knowledge, skill, and the power to follow through are also necessary. But failure to have a strong base for ministry is a guarantee that our efforts will not be as effective as they could be and may even fall short of their objective. Let's examine in more detail the various aspects of the base on which ministry rests.

1
Relation to God

Missionaries in refugee camps ministering among squalor and disease . . . Members of a storefront church doing what they can to help in the burned-out and worn-out area of a huge city . . . The Salvation Army centers scattered in places where human despair runs deepest . . . The missionary doctor who could be making a fortune in the United States but instead is pouring out his life to minister to people who "live a hundred miles beyond The Great Commission" . . . Businesswomen and professional men giving time to help lift broken lives from city ghettos . . . I've seen them all. In many cases secular co-workers who set out with them to help have long ago dropped by the wayside. The difference? God. And the Christian minister can wind up a dropout, too, if he ever forgets the importance of God.

The possibility of ministry rests not in human ability, concern, or compassion, but in God. Human efforts at ministry fail (Matt. 17:16). When the glory, the publicity, or the immediate reward is gone, the person helping others apart from God's help will usually give up and retreat.

On the other hand, the ministry resting on God's strength has staying power. Christian ministers have a sterling record of being the first to help care for difficult need. Long before modern governments were involved in foreign aid and development programs, Christian missionaries were sacrificing to help disadvantaged people throughout the world. Years before governments began to act to correct the plight of inner-city residents, Christian ministers were there helping to educate, feed, clothe, and encourage the urban poor. Pioneers in the building of hospitals, homes for orphan or neglected children, and care centers for the elderly, Christian ministers have led the way in meeting need. Before counseling became a moneymaking business, Christians were listening and caring without charge.

There is something about a Christian in ministry that makes him distinctive from the secular worker, distinctive in motivation and effectiveness. The difference is God—and the Christian's relationship to him. If he takes advantage of it, the Christian minister has resources that the secular helper simply does not have.

God's Word

God's written Word, the Bible, from beginning to end emphasizes the nature and importance of ministry. A person responsive to the Word of God will be involved in ministry. The Bible is too much of a ministry-centered book for there to be any other valid response to it.

The story the Bible tells is a story of ministry. God created the world and human life and then began to minister to the world that he had made and the life he had created. Genesis records how God met the needs of Adam and Eve. Even when they sinned and rebelled, he continued to minister to them.

From the patriarch Abraham, God fashioned a people through whom he would bless the world. He instructed them how to be a ministering people, providing specific commandments on care for the poor, the powerless, the oppressed, the needy, the weak. (See, for example, Lev. 19:9-15.) The people of the Old Testament may not have always been true to their ministry mission, but they did understand what was expected of them. (See, for example, Job 31:16-23.)

In the New Testament, revelation after revelation from God describes the importance of ministry. For example, the Book of James declares, "Pure religion and undefiled before God and the Father is this, To visit the fatherless and widows in their affliction, and to keep himself unspotted from the world" (Jas. 1:27). Further, "If a brother or sister be naked, and destitute of daily food, And one of you say unto them, Depart in peace, be ye warmed and filled; notwithstanding ye give them not those things which are needful to the body; what doth it profit?" (Jas. 2:15-16). And 1 John states: "But whoso hath this world's good, and seeth his brother have need, and shutteth up his bowels of compassion from him, how dwelleth the love of God in him?" (1 John 3:17).

Not only will a careful reading of the Bible give us a solid base for understanding the importance as well as the how-to of ministry as seen in God's instructions and commandments, it will also teach us about the relationship to ministry of God's nature, God's Son, and God's Spirit.

God's Nature

Everything we know about God points to his concern for meeting the needs of persons, that is, for ministry. Because God's being is characterized by grace and mercy, the Bible is filled with records of his acts of ministry. Sometimes he is seen ministering directly to human need, for example, guiding his people through the wilderness and feeding them with manna from heaven. Most of the time he ministers through others, instructing and empowering them to meet the needs of people. But whether directly or indirectly, God acts mercifully to care for human hurt. The Bible indicates that we are to act in a similar manner, to be like God insofar as it is humanly possible. Jesus said, "Be ye therefore perfect, even as your Father which is in heaven is perfect" (Matt. 5:48).

God is also righteous and just, bringing judgment on those who fail to live up to the standards of love, mercy, honesty, and integrity. God expects people to treat others fairly. When they do not, he acts in righteous judgment. Not only does he judge those who disobey the rules for human life, he also sends his ministers to correct the injustice and to right the wrong which is hurting people as well as to minister to those who are hurting. The Bible records that God sent his ministers, such as Amos, Micah, and Jeremiah, to attempt to clean up corrupt economic and political systems. He also used his messengers to help bind up the brokenhearted, comfort the desolate, and heal the sick and injured (Isa. 61:1-3). Sometimes we think of ministry only as helping individuals who have been hurt. That is not God's way. His way is also to deal with what is causing the hurt, with social injustice and the malfunction of economic and political systems.

God is a God of grace and stands ready to redeem and forgive those who will come to him in repentance and faith. Because he is a God of redemption, he sent his Son to die for our sins in order that we might come to salvation through faith in Jesus. God ministers to us through redemption, and through redemption he sets us on a career of ministry. A call to salvation is a call to ministry (Eph. 2:10). When we come to God through faith in Jesus Christ we find our lives being changed from self-serving to other-serving.

God is absolute power and perfect love. Because of this combination we are able to go forth and minister with confidence. The absolute power of God is demonstrated in many ways. Creation itself is testimony to his power—a billion burning suns flung into space as far as human probes can reach—and beyond. But his power is best seen in the resurrection of Jesus. Prior to Christ's resurrection death appeared invincible, all powerful. All of nature moved from life to death, from birth to decay. Nothing seemed to withstand death until Jesus came, lived, died, and was resurrected. Now for those who trust in Jesus, all of nature is reversed. The people of faith move from death to life. Dead in sin they come alive in Christ with a life which is eternal. Jesus said, "I am the resurrection, and the life: . . . whosoever liveth and believeth in me shall never die" (John 11:25-26). Those who believe in the resurrection have entered into an entirely different order of existence. They have experienced the ultimate power of God—to turn death into life.

But absolute power apart from love could be terrifying, not comforting. Can you imagine living in the presence of One who was all-powerful and had no love, no concern? God has displayed his love in an endless variety of ways. Most clearly he has demonstrated it in the gift of his Son. Christ's death on the cross is the ultimate expression of God's love. "For God so loved the world that he gave his only begotten Son, that whosoever believeth in him should not perish, but have everlasting life" (John 3:16).

It is important for love and power to go together. Many a night I have gone into the darkened room where our little daughters slept and prayed over them in love. Although not perfect, my love for them is deep and strong. Yet my own wisdom and strength is limited. Regardless of how much I love them, I could never adequately protect them or care for them. In the face of the worst that life has to throw at them, I am powerless. Yet often as I prayed I was aware that another was present—One who does not slumber or sleep, One who is all-powerful as well as all-loving. Because we had placed our lives in his hands, I could rest content.

Absolute power plus perfect love provides the possibility for complete trust. As we trust him, he sets us free from anxiety and fear, sets us free to serve and to minister. In him we learn ministry is no sideline; it is the heart of our lives. Through him we discover the resources to carry out the purpose for our lives—to serve others to his glory.

God's Son

The most complete revelation we have of what God is like is in his Son, Jesus Christ. Jesus said, "He that hath seen me hath seen the Father" (John 14:9). And Paul wrote to the Colossians, "For in him dwelleth all the fullness of the Godhead bodily" (Col. 2:9). John's Gospel declares, "In the beginning was the Word, and the Word was with God, and the Word was God . . . And the Word was made flesh, and dwelt among us . . ." (John 1:1,14). That single statement sets the Christian faith apart from all other religions and philosophies. In them the word remains word,—"Let me tell you how to live,"—but in Christ the Word was made flesh and dwelt among us—"Let me show you how to live."

A close examination of what was recorded about Jesus' actions and teachings indicates how ministry-saturated they were. Over and over again Jesus taught his disciples that they were to be ministers, servants, helpers. In his teachings he showed how closely ministry and judgment were related. (See especially Matt. 25:31-46.) By his example Jesus showed indeed that he had come "to minister, and to give his life a ransom for many" (Mark 10:45). He spent his days preaching and teaching to meet spiritual needs, healing and comforting to meet physical and emotional needs. His day-by-day activity was an example of ministry.

On two special occasions Jesus highlighted the role of servant. One was during the last meal he had with the disciples before his death. He had taught them about the importance of servanthood, but they were still arguing about who would be greatest. In a group such as that of the disciples, one would have the responsibility of washing the others' feet at mealtime—a custom of that day. In wealthy households, a servant would do the task. Thus, the one washing feet was carrying out the responsibility of a servant.

But on this particular evening the disciples were in no mood to be servants. When they entered the room where they were to eat the meal, each marched past the bowl, pitcher, and towel to be used to wash the feet of the travelers. Each was so engrossed in his own concerns that he had no concern for the others. Jesus got up, took the pitcher of water and the towel, and began to wash the disciples' feet. Peter, never at a loss for words, blurted out, in effect, "What are you doing? Surely you are not going to wash my feet?" When he realized Jesus indeed intended to wash his feet, he exclaimed, "Thou shalt never wash my feet!" Jesus replied, "If I wash thee not, thou hast no part with me." Then Peter allowed Jesus to wash his feet. Following the washing, Jesus taught the disciples once more about servanthood. If he, the Lord, was willing to minister, they ought also to be willing (John 13:3-17).

The towel and washbowl could have become the symbol of the Christian faith—a symbol of ministry. But it did not because another symbol even more profoundly demonstrated servanthood—the cross. Jesus' death on the cross was not only an act of love but also an act of servanthood. In the first-century world, Roman citizens, the wealthy, and the aristocrats did not normally endure execution by crucifixion. That was a horrible form of death reserved for criminals and slaves. Thus, not only was Jesus' death an act of ministry—to redeem us from our sin—but the form of his death, on the cross by crucifixion, was a symbol of servanthood. In his life and in his death Jesus both taught and demonstrated the servant way of life.

In contrast, we are not prone to be servants. Our selfishness and stubbornness, our pride and self-centeredness, rebel at the idea of servanthood. We much prefer to be served rather than to serve, to be ministered to rather than to minister. Clearly, a radical transformation in our nature is called for if we are to follow Jesus' pattern. And that is exactly what our Lord has provided.

In his death on the cross, he paid the penalty for our sin so that if we believe in him we are set free from the power and penalty of that sin. No longer bound by our sinfulness, we are free to live his kind of life.

But he goes a step further. He promises that if we invite him into our lives he will come live with us and help us to be ministers and servants. Following his resurrection it is possible for him to be with all believers all the time. Thus, he promises that if we are faithful to his commission to minister to the world that he will be with us always, even to the end (Matt. 28:20). The risen Lord also declared, "Behold, I stand at the door, and knock; if any man hear my voice, and open the door, I will come in to him, and will sup with him, and he with me" (Rev. 3:20). Clearly, if we invite the living Lord into our lives he will come live in us and through us, empowering us to carry out the ministry that he has set before us. One who had experienced just that, the great missionary apostle Paul, declared on the basis of his experience, "I can do all things through Christ which strengtheneth me" (Phil. 4:13).

Furthermore, he promised to come again and take us to be with him. It is the hope of his coming that keeps us at the task of ministry even when things seem hopeless. Without the hope of his coming we would be prone to give up. In fact, the basic emphasis in the Bible on Christ's coming again is on our being faithful to the task he has given us—to minister and serve—in order to be prepared for his coming (2 Pet. 3:10-14).

Clearly one part of the base for our ministry is God's Son. Through incarnation he taught us by word and by deed that we were to be ministers. Through crucifixion he opened up the possibility of our being liberated from our sinful, selfish nature in order to begin to live a life of unselfish service. Because of his resurrection he is able to indwell us, giving us the power to become what he has shown us we should be— servants. And in the promise of his coming again he gives us the hope which enables us to remain faithful to our calling, the calling to service and ministry.

God's Spirit

The Holy Spirit is necessary for productive ministry. In fact, Jesus taught that the Holy Spirit is a minister (John 14:16-26). Being himself a minister, the Holy Spirit within us fashions our lives into lives of service and ministry. The Bible promises that every believer has the aid of the indwelling Spirit. Romans, for example, declares, "But ye are not in the flesh but in the Spirit, if so be that the Spirit of God dwell in you. Now if any man have not the Spirit of Christ, he is none of his. . . . For as many as are led by the Spirit of God, they are the sons of God" (Rom. 8:9,14). Our opportunity is to open our lives more and more to the ministry of the Spirit so that we ourselves can become more useful ministers.

The Holy Spirit aids our ministry in many ways. For example, he breaks down the walls of prejudice that keep us from ministering to all persons. The early Christians had a problem with prejudice, as most of us do. The Book of Acts is largely the story of how the Holy Spirit broke down walls of prejudice. The Jewish believers at first thought of Christ as their own personal Jewish Messiah. It was only through the ministry of the Holy Spirit that they began to understand that Christ was for the whole world. Peter, one of the most prejudiced of the disciples, through the ministry of the Spirit was finally able to declare, "I perceive that God is no respecter of persons" (Acts 10:34). He made this declaration after he had seen the Holy Spirit active in the life of Cornelius, a Gentile.

The Holy Spirit also altered the attitude of Gentiles. When Paul, the missionary-apostle, was thrown in jail in Philippi, the Gentile jailer had opportunity to hear the gospel and was converted. Following his conversion, he took Paul into his home, ate with him, and treated his wounds—wounds which he himself had inflicted. As we open our lives to the Holy Spirit, he will teach us to love and care for all persons and will batter down the barriers which stand in the way of our ministering to people.

The Holy Spirit also bestows power and ability on believers to carry out ministry. The concepts of the indwelling Christ and of the indwelling Spirit are used almost interchangeably in the New Testament, each promising assistance in carrying out our ministry.

Furthermore, the Holy Spirit serves as a guide, directing us toward those who are in need of ministry. The guiding function of the Spirit is clearly seen in the Book of Acts in the life of Paul the missionary. With an entire world to tell about Jesus, he could not go everywhere at once.

The Spirit directed him where to go. Similarly, the Spirit will direct us in our ministry.

I recall vividly a postsermon conversation at Glorieta Conference Center on this point. Having preached on our responsibility to minister, I was confronted by a man who said, "You laid a guilt trip on us, but you did not tell us how to resolve it. You told us to minister, but there is more need in this world than I can meet. How do I know what to do?" After a lively and helpful conversation, we agreed that the missing ingredient in what I had preached was the function of the Spirit as a guide in ministry. We need his help to show us which of many needs we are to meet.

The most important element in our foundation for ministry is God and our relation to him. Knowing and responding to his written Word, believing in and patterning life after our Heavenly Father, trusting and obeying God's Son, being open and responsive to God's Spirit provide much of the base on which our ministry should rest.

2
Relation to Self

Marie Owen, a member of a church I pastored, saw to it that food was taken to bereaved families. She had done this for years and could always be counted on. A former pastor told me he had tried again and again to be first at the home of a grief-stricken family, but she was always there before him. And that was only one of the ministries she performed.

When she turned eighty, instead of complaining about old age she said, "I'm glad to be eighty. It sounds so dignified!" I asked her one day, "How do you accomplish as much as you do? Don't you have any aches or pains to slow you down?" I'd never heard her complain. She replied lightheartedly, "Oh, I hurt somewhere most of the time, but I find I hurt less helping someone than just sitting around feeling sorry for myself."

Unfortunately many ministers are not as persistent and consistent as Marie Owen. Some are unreliable and undependable. Others start and then quit altogether—discouraged, tired, or disillusioned. As a result, those who need their ministry are harmed by their instability.

Basic to constructive ministry is a reliable God-directed person. A ministry is as stable as the person performing it. A number of factors contribute to this stability—sound health, a realistic awareness of one's strengths and weaknesses, and a strong sense of purpose in the will of God.

Healthy

Sound health—physical, emotional, mental, and spiritual—is a tremendous asset to a minister. Some seem more naturally healthy than others, but all of us can work to be as healthy as possible.

Physical health is both a gift and a product of disciplined living. Some people are born with extraordinarily sound bodies, whereas others are plagued with numerous ailments and malfunctions. We have no control over the bodily characteristics we inherit, but we have much to do with how well we keep our bodies in shape for ministry.

The Scripture teaches that the body is the temple of the Holy Spirit (1 Cor. 6:19). We have a responsibility to see that our body is suitable for the residence of such a marvelous inhabitant. A temple that is run-down, ill-maintained, and dirty dishonors the deity worshiped in it. Likewise a body overweight, out-of-shape, and clogged with impurities is a dishonor to the Holy Spirit who dwells in it and to God who created it.

Good health practices are a part of our responsibility in Christ. This includes proper nutrition, consistent exercise and recreation, adequate rest and relaxation, careful sanitation, and preventive medicine. Poor health habits are poor stewardship.

God is concerned about what we eat. Many biblical passages discuss food and diet. The New Testament warns against making certain foods a religious taboo, implying we ought not to think that either avoiding or eating a particular food will make us more spiritual (Col. 2:16-23). On the other hand, the Bible warns about making a God of our stomachs and treats gluttony as a sin (Phil. 3:19). Eating too much results in being overweight, which detracts from our bodies' efficiency. Also, eating junk food, failing to eat a balanced diet, and consuming substances known to be harmful, such as fat meat, alcohol, drugs, and rich desserts, contribute to poor health and display a sinful lack of concern for the temple of the Holy Spirit.

Adequate exercise and recreation are important for good health. True, the Bible states that physical exercise profits little, but the Bible certainly does not teach against exercise (1 Tim. 4:8). In the advice to Timothy a contrast is being made between physical exercise and spiritual exercise. There is a mild reprimand for those who take excellent care of their physical bodies but neglect their souls.

Rest, relaxation, recreation, and play are vital to health. The Old Testament law provided for times of feasting and celebrating. Of course, some people get too much rest and relaxation; they make a vocation of it. On the other hand, many hardworking people do not provide the rest that their bodies need, and as a result their bodies begin to break down. The workaholic's body may go to pieces under the strain. Jesus took time to rest, and so should we.

Good sanitary habits are clearly necessary for sound health (Deut. 23:12-14). Much of the increased longevity of human life is due not so much to better medicine but to better sanitation. Cleanliness of the body, care in food preparation, good dental hygiene—all contribute to a sound body.

Some may protest that they know of people in poor health who were or are outstanding ministers. Certainly that is true. But they minister in spite of their bodies not because of them.

A healthy mind—one that is disciplined, well-informed, and pure— is a great asset in ministry. Many Scriptures point to the significance of sound mental ability: "Let this mind be in you, which was also in Christ Jesus" (Phil. 2:5). "Study to show thyself approved unto God, a workman that needeth not to be ashamed" (2 Tim. 2:15). "Come now, and let us reason together" (Isa. 1:18). "If any of you lack wisdom, let him ask of God" (Jas. 1:5).

Endeavor to discipline your mind to remember important information, to think in a logical fashion, and to concentrate, not being short-circuited by stress or abnormal circumstances. Store in your mind that which is helpful, positive, useful for life and ministry. Almost everything that enters the brain through our senses is stored there. Impure material that enters and is stored can detract from sound mental health.

One day while talking with a computer technician I commented that the computer seemed to be a great deal like the human brain. He replied, "In some ways it is, but in one way the computer is superior to the brain. A computer's memory can be cleared. The brain's cannot, apart from drastic measures such as surgery. What goes into the computer is all that you can get out. The same is true with the brain. But you can clear a computer's memory and start all over again. With a brain you're stuck with whatever you've put into it." The man's word was a significant warning. We should constantly guard the gateways to our minds, shutting out undesirable input.

Emotional well-being is also vital for ministry. The two most important ingredients of sound emotional health seem to be trusting God and accepting one's self. Jesus said, "Let not your heart be troubled: Ye believe in God, believe also in me" (John 14:1). The more we get to know God, the more we realize we can trust him because of his power and love. He will indeed take care of us. We do not have to be afraid of failure or fretful for our future. The Bible declares, "The fear of man bringeth a snare; but whoso putteth his trust in the Lord shall be safe" (Prov. 29:25).

The Greek word for *enthusiasm* means having God in us. As God fills our lives we are indeed enthusiastic, positive, loving, and hopeful. His love—perfect love—casts out our fear (1 John 4:18). We trust him to meet our needs and thus relax. As the Scripture tells us, "Be careful [anxious] for nothing; but in every thing by prayer and supplication with thanksgiving let your requests be made known unto God. And the peace of God, which passeth all understanding, shall keep your hearts and minds through Christ Jesus" (Phil. 4:6-7). The fretful, negative, gloomy person won't make much of a minister. The more we trust and love God the more we will be free of fear, anxiety, and despair and filled with love, peace, and enthusiasm, thus being better equipped for ministry.

Loving yourself is another prime ingredient for good emotional health. Why should we love ourselves? Because God tells us to. Jesus declared, "Thou shalt love thy neighbor as thyself" (Matt. 22:39). And the Bible declares that God loves us. Certainly we should not reject what God loves. In fact God has declared the extent of his love for us to be so great that he sent his Son to die for us. In light of that fact, to say that I cannot love myself is to despise God's gift.

Of course, God is talking about the right kind of love—not egotistical, proud, boastful, or selfish, but God's kind of love—love that seeks and wants the best for the subject loved. We should want to be the very best persons we can be, and that means shaping our lives according to the way of Jesus Christ. If we don't love ourselves, we will not care for ourselves, improve ourselves, or endeavor to bring our lives in line with God's standards.

Loving one's self also means accepting one's self. Of course, I will seek to be better than I am, more Christlike, more godly, more in line with God's will. But good emotional health calls for accepting my limitations, finiteness, lack of perfection, and matters that I can do little or nothing to change—my physical features, basic intelligence, genetic makeup, race, sex, place of birth. By accepting myself for who I am, by striving with God's help to make myself the best person I can become, I wipe away the basis for envy, jealousy, and self-pity.

Sound emotional health also requires learning to deal with failures and mistakes. What am I to do when I fall short? I am to seek God's forgiveness, accept it, and forgive myself. To do otherwise is to carry a load of guilt that will serve only to warp my emotional life and cripple my ministry to others. "I can never forgive myself" is a silly and damaging statement. Of course you can forgive yourself. If God, being holy, can forgive us, surely we can forgive ourselves. The Scriptures say, "If we confess our sins, he is faithful and just to forgive us our sins, and to cleanse us from all unrighteousness" (1 John 1:9).

Spiritual health is, of course, tremendously important for ministry. Spiritual wholeness begins with conversion, with being born again. It improves as we respond to God's call to discipleship, to the spiritual growth expected of us. As we respond to God's call to service and grow in our spiritual lives, we discover gifts bestowed on us for the purpose of ministry. By exercising these gifts we not only help others but develop in Christ. It is marvelous how God allows all things to work together for our good. Health and stability in the life of the minister depend on a sound spiritual life, a dynamic and growing relationship with God— believing in him, loving him, trusting him, and obeying him.

Self-Aware

Part of the foundation for ministry is being realistically aware of one's strengths and weaknesses, gifts and talents, interests and aptitudes, personality and character. This requires taking stock of personal resources and analyzing them. Once we have found Jesus Christ as Saviour and have set out to follow him in a life of servanthood, we need to be aware of our ministry resources.

Awareness of basic personality traits is very helpful. Personality characteristics may be altered with great effort, but our basic personality profile will likely be with us for life. I may wish I had the personality of another, but there's not much likelihood I will be able to change radically. Introverts through effort may become somewhat more outgoing, but they basically will remain persons who need time alone to recharge their batteries and get their bearings. The person who makes decisions by careful analysis of numerous details may wish that he could function by flashes of insight, but he likely never will. God has given us the personalities we need to accomplish tasks in his purpose. We ought not to fret about the way we are put together. Of course, if we have some traits that are disruptive or offensive we ought, with God's help, to strive to eliminate them.

Self-awareness also includes being aware of one's gifts and talents, aptitudes and abilities. The Scriptures speak of spiritual gifts which God bestows on his servants to enable them to minister to others. These gifts are for the work of the ministry (Eph. 4:8-16). Sometimes we become aware of these gifts through prayer, meditation, or worship. Or we may discover them through ministry and service.

At other times the Spirit of God seems to reveal the gifting to others in the church, and they make it known to us. This was the case with George W. Truett, the great Baptist preacher. When he was a young schoolteacher preparing to be a lawyer, the congregation of Baptist believers in Whitewright, Texas, became aware of his gifts for preaching. The Holy Spirit led the church to call him into a ministry of preaching. Surprised by the assessment of his fellow Christians, Truett struggled with his response, prayed earnestly, and concluded they were right. He entered into a lifetime of service which made him one of the best known and most loved preachers in the world. It may be our opportunity from time to time to help others discover their spiritual gifts.

An awareness of one's likes and dislikes, interests and disinterests is important. God equips us with interests and likes which will make us productive in a ministry he assigns us. That is not to say that we will not be called on to do things which are distasteful or difficult; we will. But by being aware of what we really enjoy doing, we can get an insight into where we can put much of our lives' energy for positive results.

And how does one become aware of his or her stock of personal resources? First, try many different things; be willing to take risks in new ventures. People who must always do things right or who cannot bear failure shut life down to a whimper and a crawl. Second, talk with a number of mature Christians who are functioning well in ministry. Ask them to observe and evaluate you. They may not always be right, but they will usually be helpful. Third, utilize the services of a career guidance center, preferably one staffed by Christians. Don't expect any of these approaches to reveal to you exactly what ministries you are to perform. They will not do that, but they will point you in the direction of those you can do well. Prayer and the Holy Spirit will do the rest.

God-Directed

The specific direction of ministry ought to come from God. Many will tell us what to do or call on us. Our own selfish desires will dictate direction to us. But a minister should be under the direction of God, not pulled this way and that by other people or by personal ambition.

A stable person is sensitive to God, not controlled by other people. A thousand voices will be calling for the minister's attention. A sea of hands will be extended in pleas for help. Well-meaning persons will be shoving this way and that trying to get him to undertake ministries in which they have a special interest. To be controlled by others is to be like a piece of taffy pulled in all directions. It is to have an antimissile personality.

Visiting one of our missile bases I heard an officer describe how an antimissile missile works: "If our radar picked up an incoming enemy missile, we would fire our antimissile missile in that general direction. Our missile has a built-in radar which picks up the incoming missile, a computer which adjusts the course of our missile according to the course of the enemy missile, and an explosive which will blast the enemy missile out of the sky when it gets close enough." I thought to myself, "I know a great many people like that. They simply react to others with no course of their own."

In contrast, the Christian minister has a kind of inner directedness, the Holy Spirit. God places his Spirit in every believer, a point of contact with the divine, a means by which we can be directed according to the purposes of God. Of course, it's possible to confuse the leadership of the Holy Spirit with our own wants and desires, but the more we mature in Christ, the less of a problem that will be.

Actually no one is free. The only freedom we have is the freedom to choose who our master will be. Freedom and self-destiny are illusions. Jesus told a group of followers, "If you continue in my word, then are ye my disciples indeed; And ye shall know the truth, and the truth shall make you free" (John 8:31-32). Suffering from a self-illusion common to us all, they replied, "We . . . were never in bondage to any man." Of course they were wrong. We have all been in bondage—to our fears, anxieties, lusts, selfishness—to sin. Thus Jesus replied, "I say unto you, Whosoever committeth sin is the servant of sin. And the servant abideth not in the house for ever: but the Son abideth ever. If the Son therefore shall make you free, ye shall be free indeed" (John 8:34-36).

Our only freedom from the masters which destroy is to put our lives in the hands of the Master who makes us whole. Thus we become the servants of God, servants whom Jesus calls friends (John 15:15). By following and serving Christ we discover ourselves on a road which leads to ministry and service. And God directs us in the walking of the way (Ps. 23). No longer concerned about what others may think, our lives can become steady and consistent.

Purposeful

Discover your stock of resources for ministry, put them to use according to God's direction, and be launched on a lifelong mission. And that, after all, is really what we are for, why God has given us life.

Unfortunately many people really don't know what they are for. If you don't know what something is for, you will likely neglect, misuse, or abuse it. But the purpose of an object is not always easy to know. I've discovered that in time spent with my father-in-law. An avid participant in flea markets and garage sales, he often runs across strange objects—at least strange to me—such as the brake of a three-legged windmill or a wrench used to change the tire on a Model T, picks it up and asks, "Do you know what this is for?" Usually I don't. I've often wondered what response I would get if I took a human being, placed him in front of a crowd, and asked, "Do you know what this is for?"

It is important to know what things are for and to use them according to their purpose. A watch is for telling time. Using it for driving nails would destroy the watch. Using it for stirring coffee would ruin the taste. Using it to tell direction would get you lost. So with life; we are to use it according to its purpose.

One of the reasons for instability in human life is that people do not really know what they are for. In Christian ministry we discover the purpose for life. We know who we are—children of God—and what we are for—to love God, to love others, and to love ourselves with that love expressed in service and ministry. That was Jesus' mission, and it is ours. As he said, "As my Father hath sent me, even so send I you" (John 20:21). This sense of purpose contributes to our well-being and stability.

Equipped with body, mind, emotions, and spiritual life as sound as possible, aware of our personal resources for ministry, directed by the will of God in the way we should walk, informed of our purpose and mission, we can become the kind of stable persons needed as a basis for effective ministry. Readiness for ministry calls for readiness as a person.

3
Relation to Others

It was late at night. I had had a busy day pastoring and was home resting. The phone rang, and as I picked it up I heard Del Borders, a deacon, saying, "Pastor, one of my families is in trouble. I'll come by and pick you up in a few minutes if you'll go with me to help." We had a deacon family ministry plan in our church, and usually the deacons took care of whatever problems arose among the families assigned to them. I knew this must be something special for one of our most able deacon ministers to call me. I agreed to go.

A few minutes later we pulled up in front of a house, rang the bell, and were ushered into a room heavy with hostility. I didn't know the people or the circumstances, but I began to try to minister. It soon was obvious I was making no headway. The deacon interrupted and began in a forthright, almost confrontive, way to talk to the members of the family. They responded to him. Soon the anger eased, and communication began. After prayer we left.

As we rode toward home I reflected on what had happened. The deacon and I both knew of God's concern and were both relatively stable, mature Christians. But he had succeeded, and I had failed. The difference, I believed, was in his understanding of those to whom we were ministering and my lack of understanding.

That's not the first time I have come up short of success in a ministry effort. Sometimes the failure was linked to lack of knowledge or skill, but more often it was the result of a lack of understanding of those with whom I was dealing.

Understanding people and how to relate to them is essential for constructive ministry. No amount of knowledge or skill can make up for an inadequacy at this point. We are not ready to minister until we have a basic understanding about the people we are to serve.

All Persons

All persons are potential recipients of our ministry in the name of Christ. When we follow Jesus we give up all right to choose whom we will love. He bids us love everyone. When we look at people through the lenses of God's love we do not see them as black or white, rich or poor, young or old, intelligent or retarded, but only as persons in need of love and ministry.

Persons from all races, nationalities, and language groups are to be part of our ministry. This has always been a difficult truth to act on. Most of us prefer our own kind of people. We are often uncomfortable around those who are different from us—and most of us don't like to be uncomfortable. Perhaps when Jesus said we were to deny ourselves and take up our crosses and follow him he had this in mind—we are to deny ourselves the right to choose those to whom we will minister and to pay the price of breaking through racial, ethnic, economic, cultural, and other barriers (Matt. 16:24).

This lesson of inclusiveness was hard for the first Christians to grasp. Jesus startled the disciples by ministering to persons to whom no self-respecting Jewish teacher of his time would minister—women, children, Samaritans, and Gentiles. He dropped an emotional bombshell when he said, "Ye shall be witnesses unto me both in Jerusalem, and in all Judaea, and Samaria, and unto the uttermost part of the earth" (Acts 1:8). The entire Book of Acts is the unfolding story of how the Holy Spirit led the first Christians to realize and then embody the truth that God indeed is no respecter of persons. We are still having to learn that lesson.

Persons of all ages are to be included in ministry. The old, the young, and all in between are loved by God and are to be loved by us. Some of us have affinity for one age group and some for another, but the true minister relates to all. The person who has denied self and submitted to God will not let personal dislikes stand in the way of ministry.

Persons from all classes of society, all degrees of education and culture, all levels of wealth, all positions in business and government, all occupations are the proper subjects of ministry. No one is to be excluded. Yet how prone we are to exclude.

A few years ago a church staff member and I were out calling on people. We pulled up in front of a house with an assortment of junk in the yard, a screen door banging idly in the wind, and dirty, half-naked children playing noisily on the porch. The address was on a so-called "prospect card," but we did not stop. As we drove away the staff member turned to me and said, "Those are just not our kind of people." What he said troubled me deeply.

Aren't all people to be our kind of people if we are in Christ, the One who died for all? But often we turn aside from ministry opportunity because a person is not our kind, has nothing to offer us or our church, or just doesn't seem worth our effort. Keep in mind that the Bible as a whole and Jesus' ministry in particular indicate God's special concern for the poor, the weak, and the afflicted.

Others are overlooked because they are invisible to most of us. Pockets of neglect exist everywhere. The poor often report that they seem to be invisible to the nonpoor—that we look through them instead of at them. Relating to some persons is difficult because they are traveling ghettos, specialists who move primarily with their own kind—performing artists, traveling salesmen, seamen, truckers. But all people have need, and we are to minister to all people.

Total Needs

Not only are we to minister to all persons, but we are to minister to all needs. Jesus fixed his ministry on whole people, not on bodies as some medical technicians might, or on minds as some educators do, or on emotions as some counselors and psychiatrists do, or on souls as some religionists do. He was concerned about whole people—hairy, bloody, sweaty human beings. And remember his basic command—"Follow me!" We are to follow him in ministering to whole people, to total need.

Spiritual need is primary. If we meet other needs—physical, emotional, mental—but do not meet spiritual needs, we have failed ultimately. The Bible teaches that sin has damaged us all, affecting every part of life. Sin has distorted the relationship of human beings with God, damaged the relationship of human beings with one another, destroyed the harmony God intended between the physical world and human life, and corrupted the physical world itself.

We meet spiritual needs by witnessing to others of our own experience with God through Christ, by sharing with an individual how to be saved, by teaching God's Word, and by communicating the riches of God's love. We also meet spiritual needs by encouraging persons to be part of a fellowship of believers, of a church, because people grow in spiritual strength not in isolation but in relation to others.

Physical needs are also of great importance. Jesus obviously thought so. He fed the hungry, healed the sick, and urged his disciples to do the same. He told us that we are to provide water for the thirsty, shelter for the destitute, and food for the starving. Indeed these are spiritual acts when done in the name of Christ to the glory of God. While multitudes suffer pain and illness, endure starvation, live in hovels, breathe foul air, and drink disease-inducing water, our ministry challenge to meet physical needs is enormous.

Emotional needs are also our concern. They were the concern of Jesus. He comforted the fearful, encouraged the anxious, confronted the prejudiced, visited the lonely, and forgave the guilt-ridden. All around us people suffer emotional problems, some to the extent they are hospitalized or institutionalized; but most continue to struggle on, wearing a front that keeps us from being aware of how awful their inner pain is.

Mental needs are rampant, too. Minds crippled by ignorance, twisted by superstition, blighted by perversion need our help. So do brains untrained to reason and think, rotting under the constant wash of the media's trivia. Jesus ministered through teaching, training, challenging. He pushed back the black night of superstition, and in its place injected the light of God. So should we.

Every Area

The extent of our potential territory for ministry is made clear in the Bible. It is everywhere, throughout the entire world. Jesus said, "Go ye therefore, and teach all nations" (Matt. 28:19). He declared, "Go ye into all the world" (Mark 16:15). Before his ascension he commissioned the disciples to go "unto the uttermost part of the earth" (Acts 1:8).

Ministry and missions are the threads which weave the fabric of our life in Christ. We have responsibility to minister to the total needs of all persons in every part of the earth. We cannot fulfill this responsibility apart from missions. We must be willing to go beyond our normal routine to put our lives alongside those we might not otherwise contact in order to carry out a specific task, in this case—ministry.

We are to be willing to go as ministers anywhere in the locale where we live—to offices and factories, to homes and apartments, to institutions and organizations, to slums and suburbs, to schools and bars—in short, to where people are.

Our entire nation is also an area for ministry. Although we think of the United States as a Christian land, millions of spiritually dead persons live within its borders. Throughout our country multitudes struggle with spiritual, physical, emotional, and mental needs, and they are persons for whom we have responsibility. Our land is littered with those whose lives have been broken by involvement in some form of personal sin, as well as by persons who are lonely, abused, unemployed, institutionalized, mentally ill, emotionally depressed, hungry, illiterate, and homeless. Many of these seldom come in contact with churches. We must go to them.

The entire world is the realm of our ministry responsibility. Jesus sent us there. Human need calls us there. God wants the whole world to know life through his Son. He has a plan to send his people to minister to persons everywhere. But the plan is not working. The fault is not with the plan or with God but with God's people—those of us who remain close to home rather than go on mission in God's world. Christians are clustered in enclaves scattered here or there on the earth while billions receive no real ministry from Christ's followers. None of us is really ready to minister until we are willing to go anywhere and everywhere.

Positive Approach

Our attitude toward those to whom we minister is extremely important. Love, of course, is the overarching motivation. We serve not out of duty but out of love if we serve according to God's standards. The thirteenth chapter of 1 Corinthians breaks love down into component parts. These spell out something of what we should be in relation to others if our ministry is effective.

We should approach those in need with a humble, not a haughty, spirit. We are not better, smarter, or wiser than they. We, as they, are sinners. What we are in Christ is the result of grace, a gift, and therefore no ground for pride. To approach one in need in a condescending spirit is to scuttle the possibility of effective ministry.

We are to minister encouragingly as Jesus did, not condemningly. To the woman caught in adultery he said, "Neither do I condemn thee: go, and sin no more" (John 8:11). It is difficult to resist the temptation to tell people that if they had just done this or that they would have avoided their calamity, but what they need is help, not a harangue.

Similarly, a positive rather than a negative attitude is helpful. Don't major on how bad, how wrong someone is; instead share with him what hope and possibilities can be his. God's love and power are the promises we hold out to people. Most persons suffer from low self-esteem. They are down on themselves. They doubt if anybody, including God, could really love them. Many of those to whom we minister feel depressed, guilty, and hopeless. They need positive reinforcement, not so much about how good they are—for they know better—but about how wonderful God is and how much he wants to help them.

Effective ministry is also rooted in realism. Sometimes we must tell people that things are not likely to become any better and then share with them insight on how they can possess God's power and comfort in disaster. The loss of a loved one, the deterioration of health, the prospect of enduring intense pain, the termination of a marriage—no amount of well-meant words or pious platitudes will alter these conditions. Sometimes people must be helped to face the reality that conditions beyond their control are going to cause great suffering—an economy in depression, an industry becoming obsolete, a neighborhood disintegrating, a nation going to war. It is not pie-in-the-sky-by-and-by religion to point people to the promise of heaven where God will wipe away all tears from our eyes and there will be no more pain and death (Rev. 21:4). After we've done all we can to alter injustice in society and to ease hurt in individuals, our finest ministry is to hold up the hope that belongs to those who are in Christ.

Comprehensive Strategy

Clearly the challenge of ministry is great. In order to minister to the total needs of all persons everywhere God has given us a comprehensive strategy. We are to minister—both individually and corporately—and we are to minister both to individual hurts and to group malfunctions.

God certainly wills that we minister to individuals who hurt. Most of us agree that we are to help the hungry, sick, homeless, and others mangled by life's misfortunes or society's malfunctions. But we are also to tackle the tough task of trying to prevent the hurt. Prevention as well as correction is a ministry. Sometimes we can patch up the broken bodies of persons smashed in alcohol-related automobile accidents, but we should also work to prevent such accidents from happening at all. To do this calls for working with groups, institutions, and other social structures and helping them function in a way to benefit rather than to damage human life.

God has gifted us with social structures such as homes, churches, businesses, and governments to help us meet basic human needs. The quality of life largely depends on how well these structures function. A breakdown causes hurt to many. Therefore part of our ministry is seeing that these structures function well by being a responsible part of them and by working to improve them.

Family life needs a minister's time and attention, care and planning (Eph. 5:22 to 6:4). No family thrives on neglect. Unfortunately, some people are so busy ministering to others that they have little or no time for family. That is a violation of God's priority; family came first among all the institutions. One of our best ministries may be to strengthen our own families. The by-product of that will help bring healing to a hurting world.

A church should be part of the life of a minister. Within a church a person gains insight, strength, and direction for ministry. Through church structure we are able to magnify ministry. Thus, a responsible minister will work to strengthen the church of which he is part—

participating in worship and education, contributing tithes and offerings, praying for the leadership, filling positions in the organization.

Economic structures call for responsible participation, also. The workaday world provides the necessities of life—for others and for ourselves. The Bible takes seriously the world of work, indicating that we are to do our work "as unto the Lord." By working consistently, honestly, diligently, and faithfully we minister through work (Eph. 4:28; 1 Thess. 4:9-12; 2 Thess. 3:7-13).

Governments also require responsible participants in order to function effectively, and democratic government organizations such as ours are especially in need of the support and participation of all people. God's Word stresses the importance of government, urging believers to pray for those who are in authority and to obey government officials (Rom. 13:1-7; 1 Tim. 2:1-3; 1 Pet. 2:13-17). Christians can minister in scores of ways in government.

Various community organizations also stand in need of support and involvement. Schools, recreational and leisure organizations, entities which enhance art and culture—all these contribute to the welfare of human life. Serving either as paid staff or as volunteers, we minister through these structures.

In addition to functioning within structures to help them be strong and stable, we can also minister by working from the outside to improve them. Some churches, for example, conduct programs of family enrichment to strengthen family life. Others sponsor seminars and conferences on citizenship and thus help strengthen governments.

In some cases ministry may require us to establish structures where none exist. In the settlement of our nation, for example, many Christians helped establish not only churches but also schools because there were no educational institutions. In places where the water-supply system is inadequate, Christians have moved beyond bringing cups of water to the thirsty and are busy drilling wells and setting up water-supply systems. Wherever there is an unmet need which can be met through structures, Christians have an opportunity to serve by establishing the needed structure.

A comprehensive strategy also calls for ministering both as individuals and as parts of organizations and groups. Most think of ministry in terms of one person ministering to another. This is clearly valid, but so also is corporate action. Organization to meet need was part of Jesus' pattern. He called twelve disciples and taught them. Then he assembled seventy, trained them, and sent them out two by two in ministry. When he fed the five thousand he divided the people into small groups and sent the disciples among them with food.

One reason why he gave us churches is so that we could minister more effectively. A church is able to do what an individual cannot do. The church, as the body of Christ, is made up of many individuals with different gifts for ministry. Thus a church is a multigifted body able to meet an extraordinary number of needs.

But even an individual church is not able to meet all the needs around it. That is why cooperation among churches is important. A single church is limited in ministry. Linked with others in cooperative action, a church can touch the world. A denomination of churches is not merely an expression of doctrinal differences, it is a practical means of uniting for ministry.

A comprehensive strategy also calls for general concern as well as specific action. If we are truly ready to minister, we will be willing to go to anyone anywhere to meet any need. But in order to actually minister it is necessary to concentrate on a specific person with a specific need in a specific place. We cannot do everything. Not even a denomination of churches can do that. But we must do something. Sensitive to the leadership of his Spirit, we will be able to discern God's will in regard to the specifics of ministry.

For some people this is a difficult step. It is much easier to love the world in general than to minister to someone in particular. That is why most of us prefer to daydream than to act, to plan rather than to execute. When we go into action we come face-to-face with our finiteness and limitations, and that is painful. But it is absolutely essential for ministry. In order to minister we must finally go to someone, somewhere, with a particular need and enter the role of servant.

Readiness for ministry calls for more than an urge to do good. It calls for a solid base on which to operate. That base results from a right relationship with God, ourselves, and other persons. A person is not really ready to minister until he understands the nature of those relationships and has begun to work to make them strong. All ministry rests on this foundation.

PART II
Knowledge for Ministry

A train runs on two tracks, each essential, both connected. Likewise, ministry needs two important and interrelated tracks—one of knowledge and one of skill. We need to know both *what* to do and *how* to do it in order to be effective in ministry. Part II considers the knowledge required for ministers, *what* we need to know in order to minister effectively. Part III will deal with the skills called for in ministry.

Acquiring the knowledge necessary for ministry is not a once-and-for-all achievement but a lifetime process. The Bible tells us how important knowledge is, how responsible we are to equip our minds. Jesus said that we are to love God with all of our mind. Paul wrote to a young preacher, "Study to shew thyself approved unto God" (2 Tim. 2:15). Timothy and Titus were told the importance of sound doctrine and urged to carefully teach the truth to all believers (2 Tim. 4:1-5).

The relation between knowledge and ministry is clear. If we do not know what the right thing to do is, then we are doomed to live according to ignorance and perhaps falsehood. Right action is based on correct knowledge.

Strangely enough, some ministers seem afraid of knowledge. Indeed we should fear false knowledge, but we should realize that all true knowledge comes from God (Prov. 9:10). Since God is the origin of truth, we are free to seek truth with all our might. Yet there are those who equate ignorance with spiritual power and knowledge with spiritual impotence. The fact is that many of the greatest ministers in the history of the Christian movement were persons of great learning and knowledge.

Our effectiveness in ministry will increase as our knowledge of the truth expands. It is important for us to understand both what we need to know and how we can acquire that knowledge. Certain skills, such as the following, are used to gain knowledge.

Studying is the basic method for gaining knowledge. Many schools have courses in how to study that would benefit a minister. Effective study requires concentrating, focusing attention on what is to be learned, and eliminating distractions. Good reading and writing skills are essential for study. An ability to read rapidly with high retention will enhance the minister's learning.

Observing such things as daily events, other persons, audiovisuals, and experiments helps us garner knowledge. A step beyond merely looking or seeing, observing demands concentration, memory, and reflection.

Experiencing takes us beyond the detached stance of the observer and into the action. We can learn from our experiences if we will reflect on them, squeezing meaning and insight from what happens to us that can be used in ministry.

Listening carefully is a learning skill many ministers especially need. In contrast to merely hearing, listening calls for concentration. Concentration is aided by taking notes, writing down an outline of key thoughts, recording basic facts, figures, and quotations, summarizing frequently what you have heard, and asking questions for clarification.

Remembering enables us to store knowledge for future use and can save vast amounts of time. By concentrating and memorizing we can add great quantities of material to our memory, material which we can use for constructive thought.

Contemplating is a key to gaining certain forms of knowledge, especially about ourselves, others, and interpersonal relations. Contemplation involves deep concentration on a single subject for a length of time, considering it from many different angles.

Praying is a means of acquiring knowledge, although that is by no means the only purpose of prayer. Prayer is both an aid to other methods of learning and a method in itself. While at prayer many Christians have received insight into the Christian life and gained knowledge about God and his ways with us.

The following chapters discuss the areas of knowledge a minister needs to master, the attitudes which enhance the acquiring of knowledge, and the resources available for learning. Ministers in so-called religious vocations may need more depth than other people in some of these areas, but the ministry of all will be enhanced by learning.

4
Areas of Knowledge

Most persons who are skilled in preparing others for ministry insist that those who serve in Christ's name need a knowledge of God, of the world, of people, and of how to relate other people to God. Some ministers need knowledge of special subjects for particular tasks. At first glance, the amount of knowledge required seems absolutely overwhelming. But remember, no one acquires it all, even in a lifetime. And that which we gain comes over many years.

Consider the outline of these areas of knowledge as something of a chart, indicating where we are to go on a long journey. Just as a journey is broken down into segments, so the knowledge needed for ministry is to be obtained in pieces over a period of time.

The Knowledge of God

What we know about God is what he chooses to reveal. The primary source of knowledge about God is, therefore, the Bible because the Bible is the record of God's revelation of himself. The writers of the Bible were inspired by the Holy Spirit to record these revelations, and thus, in a sense, the Bible is God's revelation to us.

Other persons preserved the record, passing it down from generation to generation, often at great sacrifice. Scholars paid the price to learn the biblical languages and to translate them into other languages so that people throughout the world now have access to the knowledge of God through the Bible. All of us owe a great debt to Christian scholars and teachers.

The study of the Bible is essential for a knowledge of God. Sometimes we are prone to study more about the Bible than we are to study the Bible itself.

That is a mistake. The Christian minister should carefully study the Scriptures, seeking knowledge about God, his nature, and his will.

The study of the Bible will be enhanced by acquiring certain tools for biblical study. For example, an acquaintance with ancient history and cultures helps us to understand the Bible. So also does a study of the ancient languages in which the Bible is written—Hebrew, Aramaic, and Greek. An understanding of how the sixty-six books of the Bible were written, preserved, collected into one book, and translated is useful.

The primary history of God's working with his world and people is found in the Bible, but the study of archaeology and ancient history provides additional insights. Church history, the record of God's work with his people since the closing of the biblical period, aids our understanding also.

Theology, an academic discipline devoted to the study of God, provides us assistance in knowing about God. The primary source book for theology is the Bible. Theology is usually divided into three basic areas of study. Biblical theology is a study of the various themes and emphases of the Bible. Systematic theology organizes the various teachings of the Bible according to subjects. Historical theology traces beliefs about certain doctrines through various periods of history.

Every minister has a theology—but sometimes it is a hand-me-down from someone else. It is important for a minister to develop a theology for himself, carefully working through the biblical material and the thoughtful writings of other Christians. In this way, the knowledge of God which he acquires by study will become part of the warp and woof of his own life.

Some Christians believe that they can know a great deal about God through the study of science or the use of reason. Although a reverent study of natural science and the application of reason can help us formulate concepts of God, these remain a far inferior path to the knowledge of God than the Scriptures. Sometimes termed natural theology, they should at best be considered supplementary.

Other Christians insist that they have a direct knowledge of God which comes through prayerful meditation or introspection by which they discover a divine spark within them. Numerous sincere mystics through the ages have claimed to have experienced special direct encounters with God and to have come to know him in this way. Many have insisted they could not put such knowledge into words because it was beyond human expression.

In order to evaluate their authenticity, such divine encounters must be placed alongside the biblical revelation as a benchmark. Otherwise anyone professing such a special revelation could claim an insight into the knowledge of God for which there would be no basis of evaluation. Most Christians believe that God is consistent and that he will not reveal himself in a personal encounter in any way contrary to how he has revealed himself through his Word. After all, the most complete revelation of God that we have is in Jesus Christ, and the Bible is our only adequate record of the life and teachings of Jesus.

Knowledge About the World

Knowledge of the world in which we live—both the physical and social aspects—is necessary for effective ministry. It enables us to understand the setting in which we minister as well as the causes for human hurt.

The Bible is the source of basic knowledge about the world and its people. The Bible provides answers to such questions as, Who created the world? Why was the world created? What is the purpose of life and existence? How can the fragmented disorder of the world be restored to wholeness? Answers to questions such as these are found in the Bible.

God created all that is. God sustains what he has created, and without his care it would cease to be. Life itself is a gift from God. Thus all that we are and all that we have comes from God.

We are not owners; we are stewards of God's creation. As you minister, remember that God has all the resources he needs to accomplish his purposes in his world. As I have anguished over where to find resources to meet human need, I have reminded myself that all the resources necessary belong to God. But when I take stock of the pitiful resources which we who minister have at our disposal to care for the hurt of the world, I realize we do not have enough. Why? Because sin has affected

God's world, and sinful people refuse to use God's money and resources—for which they are stewards—to meet need. Sin has not only created the need, but it has also thwarted the efforts of God's ministers to meet that need.

This means that ministers will fight big battles with short sticks. As a friend of mine said, "It's like charging hell with a thimbleful of water." Or another, living in a forest area of the West, said, "It's like fighting a forest fire with a wet sack." It is hard not to be frustrated and disillusioned, but those reactions create no positive results. Instead we ought to acknowledge the awful effect of sin on the world, use the resources we have, and pray that somehow those who have been selfish will begin to share.

Other helpful sources of knowledge about the world are available, such as history, sociology, philosophy, economics, political theory, and the various branches of science. Each of these disciplines has amassed enormous volumes of material, some of it from a materialistic or secular point of view. Although the Christian minister can learn from all such sources, it is important to be aware of the presuppositions. These disciplines are especially helpful to the Christian minister in throwing light on the impact that the physical world and the structures of society have on human life.

Another source of information are studies about the problems and crises in our world. News of current events often spotlight places where vast needs exist. By keeping abreast of the news we are made aware of where social systems are breaking down, how people are hurting, where ministry ought to be directed. Admittedly, obtaining objective news is difficult. We should get information on current events from a wide variety of sources and from different perspectives. Somewhere in all of the information, as contradictory as it might appear, there is likely to be an indication of how things really are.

Knowledge About People

The bottom line of ministry is helping people, and a knowledge of people is mandatory if we are to minister to their needs effectively. We ought to know what needs people have, why they have them, and how they can be met.

Again, the Bible is a basic source for knowledge about people. The Scriptures tell us about the source of human life, the purposes for that life, and the cause for our basic difficulties—sin and alienation from God. The Bible indicates the nature of human life—that we are not merely material beings but have also a spiritual dimension, that we are created in the image of God. The Bible also presents basic information on the responsibilities of persons for one another and how we are to relate to each other in social systems such as family, work, government, and church. The Scriptures contain the basic prescription for man's ailments—a faith in and love for God, love and respect for one another, love and acceptance of one's self.

Other disciplines, such as psychology, sociology, social psychology, physiology and anatomy, anthropology, and logic, produce information which can be useful to the Christian minister. Literature, drama, and history provide insight into the ways people think and relate to one another.

By carefully studying these disciplines the Christian can garner a wealth of knowledge to help in serving others. Secular experts in these fields may operate from presuppositions alien to ours, but their findings can nevertheless be useful in ministry. Remember that all such knowledge is tentative, subject to revision and change as new data is encountered. Current ideas on how the brain functions, for example, are vastly different from those of one hundred years ago.

Knowledge About Relating

In addition to a knowledge about God, the world, and people, a knowledge of how to relate the world and its people to God is vital to effective ministry. A number of areas of study such as evangelism, ministry, ethics, and missions are available to aid us in this task.

The study of evangelism brings together information from the Bible, theology, and psychology to help us understand how to share the gospel with lost persons. Missions relates evangelism to the entire world. It is a discipline that collects knowledge about how persons everywhere can be brought face-to-face with the claims of Christ. Missions also includes the study of other cultures and religions.

Christian social ethics deals with how people ought to relate to one another and how society ought to be structured. Ethics also considers how we are to change the structures of society to bring them more in line with the purposes of God. To do that requires not only a knowledge of God and his ways with people but also an understanding of current events, economics, political science, sociology, social psychology, and various approaches to social change.

The field of Christian ministry delves into how we are to relate God's love to the hurts of people in his world. That calls for a knowledge of why people hurt—knowledge from physiology, psychology, theology—and how those hurts can be alleviated. Just as there is not one medicine that takes care of all disease, neither is there one ministry that takes care of all human hurt and distress. Specific problems call for specific remedies. And yet all efforts stem from the same motive—a love for people in the name of Christ.

Knowledge About Special Subjects

Because of the wide variety of human hurt and need, special knowledge is needed to deal with certain problems. Entire occupations center around meeting particular needs. These occupations require a great deal of technical training. For example, Christian counselors need intensive training to equip them to deal with mental and emotional problems. Family counselors should have extensive study about family life and how to enrich it. Physicians need lengthy training to care for diseases of the human body. Where highly specialized knowledge is required to care for human need, Christian ministers must acquire it if they are called to meet that need.

Specialty knowledge is also mandated by certain locations of ministry. When a Christian minister is directed by God to serve outside his native culture, then he must learn a new language, new customs, and new ways of relating. Those ministering in institutions such as prisons, hospitals, and children's homes need to learn about the specialized environments in which they serve. Acquiring such knowledge is one of the prices some must pay to be ready to minister.

Faced with such a staggering body of knowledge to be mastered, a person is tempted to ask, "Can I minister without knowing all that?" The answer is, "Of course you can. But the better you are prepared and the more you know, the better you are able to minister." And since we serve the King of kings, shouldn't we want to do the very best job of ministry possible? I think so. And how are we to go about acquiring the knowledge required? That's what the next two chapters are about.

5

Attitudes for Gaining Knowledge

Even after teaching for several years as a seminary professor, I never grew accustomed to the fact that in almost every class a number of students would barely get by and some would fail; others would do very well, however. They all attended the same classes, read the same books, wrote papers on the same subjects, entered the same discussions, but some came out with knowledge and some didn't. What was the difference? It was not always a difference in intelligence or background or experience. The difference had to do primarily with the student's attitude and approach to learning. Those who were well-disciplined and open to learning, with a keen sense of purpose and priority, gained the most.

Readiness to minister requires knowledge. And gaining knowledge requires a readiness to learn. Few things are as important in preparing for ministry as having the right attitude and approach to learning.

Reverence

Since all truth and helpful knowledge come from God, we should approach the learning process with reverence. In a sense we are on holy ground. What we are dealing with comes from God; it is a part of his revelation to us, a portion of his expression of love for us.

My first semester as a seminary student was a very painful experience for me because of the lack of reverence I encountered on the part of some of the students. My undergraduate study had been in a secular state university where Christian students, in a minority, lived as on a mission field. We had a great deal of fun in our Christian fellowship, but we took very seriously our mission and the tools which we used to carry it out—particularly the Bible. In seminary I encountered students who seemed to have very little respect for the Bible, Christian doctrine, or for that matter, the professors, all of whom dealt reverently with the Bible and Christian truth. These students made jokes about subjects which are no joking matter, such as hell, and treated the Scriptures lightly, even flippantly. Many of them were successful young preachers and youth evangelists. I thought perhaps one had to behave in such a fashion to be successful in ministry, and that troubled me a great deal. But I also observed other students who took a reverent approach to the knowledge we were to acquire for ministry. Having observed many ministers for many years, I am convinced that reverence in the face of truth to be learned is important.

Humility

Humility is a virtue commendable in anyone but essential for adequate learning. Humility is not a doormat demeanor but a clear recognition of one's limitations and needs. Paul wrote to the Corinthians, "Let no man deceive himself. If any man among you seemeth to be wise in this world, let him become a fool, that he may be wise" (1 Cor. 3:18). If we take realistic stock of what we know in contrast to what we need to know, we will all feel insufficient.

In such a humble state we are capable of being helped. As James wrote, "Wherefore he saith, God resisteth the proud, but giveth grace unto the humble . . . Humble yourselves in the sight of the Lord, and he shall lift you up" (Jas. 4:6,10). Micah included humility as one of the requirements of true religion: "He hath shewed thee, O man, what is good; and what doth the Lord require of thee, but to do justly, and to love mercy, and to walk humbly with thy God?" (Mic. 6:8).

Jesus provided a vivid illustration of the importance of humility when he taught, "Except ye be converted, and become as little children, ye shall not enter into the kingdom of heaven. Whosoever therefore shall humble himself as this little child, the same is greatest in the kingdom of heaven" (Matt. 18:3,4). Most children make great learners because they are quick to say, "I don't know; teach me." Often pride gets in the way of adults, and we are ashamed to admit that we do not know. The person who in this sense becomes as a little child is ready to learn.

Desire

Humility causes us to say, "I don't know." Needed also is the desire to learn which causes us to say, "And I want to know." The minister must hunger and thirst after knowledge, eager to learn everything possible in order to be more effective in ministry. Reverence, humility, and desire— these are the big three. When they are present in a person's life, he will practically always gain whatever knowledge he needs in order to serve. Fred Dea exhibited all three when he came to California with his wife, Lillian, to help start churches. Retired, in his late sixties, he had no formal training for the task, but by working with missionaries and taking seminary courses he learned what he needed to know. He led in beginning a new church.

A strong desire to learn seems to stem from two basic insights: a realization of how desperate and needy people really are and an awareness of how clearly God has commanded us to minister to those who hurt. People who have peered into the depth of human despair and have drunk deeply of God's grace realize the urgency of ministry and want to acquire all of the knowledge possible in order to serve well.

Discipline

Normally, discipline is closely linked with a desire to learn. The person who wants desperately to acquire knowledge will discipline himself to gain it, realizing there is a price to be paid. Knowledge does not come easily or automatically. Time, concentration, and often money are required. If people are willing to discipline themselves to pay the price for knowledge in other fields—medicine, law, banking, architecture, athletics—surely we should be willing to pay the price to acquire knowledge for ministry.

After all, no task is more important than carrying out the mission of Christ and ministering to others in his name. The physician's work is important, but the medical team deals with bodies which are doomed to dust. Those who minister to the whole person in Christ's name deal with eternal life. The lawyer's task is significant, but an attorney handles the laws of men, which are fated to fade. Christ's servants handle the Law and Word of God, of which not one jot or tittle will fade away. Architects, engineers, and contractors carry out vital tasks in constructing cities for our habitation, but those cities will ultimately crumble to rubble. Those who minister to the needs of people to the glory of God, on the other hand, guide them toward a city not constructed by human hands but whose maker and builder is God (Heb. 11:10), the eternal city not blighted by night, or tears, or pain (Rev. 21:1-4).

If people are willing to discipline themselves for years of intensive study, gaining great blocks of knowledge for such professions, shouldn't we be willing to spend at least as much effort, display at least as much discipline, in acquiring the knowledge necessary for effective ministry?

Discrimination

With an abundance of material available in practically every area of knowledge, we cannot give attention to all of it. We must be discriminating, picking and choosing what is best.

But how are we to know what to major on and what to avoid? The Scriptures indicate that we are to stay away from uselessly disruptive matters: "But foolish and unlearned questions avoid, knowing that they do gender strifes" (2 Tim. 2:23). "But avoid foolish questions, and genealogies, and contentions, and strivings about the law; for they are unprofitable and vain" (Titus 3:9).

We should generally concentrate on material from people whose lives demonstrate a close walk with Christ, avoiding that of those persons who obviously fall far short of Christ's standards. As the epistle of Titus records, "There are many unruly and vain talkers and deceivers, specially they of the circumcision: Whose mouths must be stopped, who subvert whole houses, teaching things which they ought not, for filthy lucre's sake" (Titus 1:10-11). Paul appealed to his reputation as a basis for believing his teachings (2 Tim. 3:10-11).

We can also discriminate on the basis of the presuppositions behind material. Is it based on a deep commitment to the reality of God, the truth that is in Jesus Christ, the veracity of the Bible? Or does it seem to be based more on a materialistic world view? We need to know what non-Christians believe and are teaching, but we should realize they are looking at life from a different point of view and are committed to different presuppositions than we.

A helpful rule of thumb in selecting material is to obtain it from sources you believe are trustworthy either from your own personal experience or the testimony of others. Certain publishers, conference centers, authors, teachers, schools, and other sources of information have sterling reputations. It is possible to get a less than desirable bit of material from the best of sources, but by and large you can count on resources from such sources being helpful.

Determining priorities helps the discriminating person in a pursuit of knowledge. We can't learn everything; we can't even study everything. We must concentrate on a few matters at a time. Priority has two dimensions—what we do first and what we do most. Each is important in the matter of obtaining knowledge.

Jesus emphasized the importance of priority in regard to putting first things first. He said, "Seek ye first the kingdom of God, and his righteousness; and all these things shall be added unto you" (Matt. 6:33). We are really not ready for ministry until we have put God first in our lives—the knowledge of God, service of God, obedience to the will of God. Thus in preparation for ministry a person should begin by studying the Bible, concentrating on the portions of Scripture that deal with the nature and purpose of God. Then a person should move to a study of creation—the world and its people. He should proceed next to the knowledge that deals with how God relates to his world and how we are to relate God's purpose to our life. Finally, the minister should strive to acquire the special knowledge needed for those special ministries to which he feels led.

Priority is to some extent determined by process or prerequisites. For example, in most colleges and universities certain upper-level courses have prerequisites—lower-level courses which are required before you can take the advanced ones. A similar principle applies to all learning. We must begin with the simple and move toward the more complex.

Paul wrote to the early Christians that he had fed them with milk because they were not yet ready for the meat of the Word (1 Cor. 3:2).

Thus it is wise to begin studying the simplest, most basic Scriptures, doctrines, and subjects. Deal with particulars only after you have the broad picture in mind. Get in mind the basic history of God's dealing with his people before you delve into the details of various portions of that history. Too many people do not know who came first—Moses or Abraham, Isaiah or David—and thus they are in perpetual confusion as they endeavor to study the Bible. Establish priorities—get the basics, the fundamentals, the overall picture, the elementary material in mind before proceeding.

Priority also has to do with what you concentrate on the most. Admittedly, many of us prefer the simple to the complex, frothy to meaty material. We are prone to linger long over that which is intriguing, titillating, or amazing. Many of us had rather spend our time on matters about which we can do little or which require little response from us—perhaps a form of escapism. Have you noticed how some Christians will spend hours and hours studying prophecy concerning the future—a matter about which we can do little—but hardly give any attention to missions—a matter about which we can do much?

How then can we determine what areas of knowledge deserve priority in regard to time and effort? First, major on basic information, doctrines, and subject matter, not on peripheral items. Second, give attention to what is most solidly established rather than on what is primarily speculative. Third, concentrate on the special ministries God leads you to carry out.

Purpose

Acquiring knowledge ought to be for a worthwhile purpose. The Christian minister gains knowledge for the purpose of using it to serve God and others. Some people treat learning as recreation—they are forever wanting to read this, study that, discuss the other, without ever coming to any conclusion or moving to any action. The Bible talks about such people: "For of this sort are they which creep into houses, and lead captive silly women laden with sins, led away with divers lusts, Ever learning, and never able to come to the knowledge of the truth" (2 Tim. 3:6-7).

In acquiring knowledge we need constantly to ask ourselves, "How can I use this to serve God? How can I utilize this to minister to others?" One of the reasons why learning best takes place while engaged in ministering is that the practice of ministry keeps us rooted to reality. However, beware of judging too quickly the practical uselessness of certain material. If we place ourselves under the supervision of mature, experienced ministers, they will provide us with the material we will need for the future even though we may not need it now. In that case we'll be in a position akin to the disciples when Jesus said to them at the washing of their feet, "What I do thou knowest not now; but thou shalt know hereafter" (John 13:7).

We must continually remind ourselves that the purpose for acquiring knowledge is ministry. Otherwise we may become pathetic creatures who are always studying the Bible but never doing what it says, perpetually conversing about Christ but never carrying out his mission.

Armed with the proper attitudes for learning—reverence, humility, desire, discipline, discrimination, purpose—a person is ready to deal with resources for acquiring the knowledge necessary for ministry. The next chapter deals with these matters.

6
Resources for Acquiring Knowledge

"Daddy, what do you want to be when you grow up?" is a question Meredith and Allison, our daughters, have often asked, with good reason. God has allowed me to do many different jobs. In my school years I worked as a janitor, drove trucks, sold brushes from door to door, labored on bridges, sold magazines, assisted in an accountant's office, pastored, and preached youth revivals. Following graduation from seminary I have served as a denominational employee, seminary professor, pastor, seminary president, and executive director of a Baptist state convention, in that order, within twenty years.

Seriously, I am grateful for God's leading me into various places of service. I have enjoyed and benefited from each. I have discovered that the basic ministry skills are transferable; I've not had to start all over in each position. Many of the same skills are required for teaching, pastoring, administrating, and managing. But I've discovered the body of knowledge required for each of these positions is quite different.

Through the years I have been required to be a continuing learner, attempting to master various areas of knowledge. This has made me acutely aware of the numerous resources available for the minister on pilgrimage. I've utilized most of them. They are available to all who are striving to be ready to minister.

Because our avenues and locations of ministry change, most of us must be constantly preparing to minister. And since we do not know when God is going to call us in a different direction, we need to maintain an up-to-date inventory of the resources available for getting the knowledge we will need.

In utilizing the resources described in this chapter various methods of learning are available, such as lectures, conversations, dialogues, debates, panels, symposiums, role playing, case studies, experiments, and testing. Highly developed learning skills, such as studying, reading, and listening, plus good attitudes for learning, will be a big asset to the minister in getting the most out of these resources.

Individuals

A Christian more mature and experienced than ourselves can provide us a wealth of knowledge. Paul used such an approach with Timothy: "Thou therefore, my son, be strong in the grace that is in Christ Jesus. And the things that thou hast heard of me among many witnesses, the same commit thou to faithful men, who shall be able to teach others also" (2 Tim. 2:1-2). If we are indeed humble, it should cause us no discomfort to approach another and say, "I need to learn from you. Will you teach me?"

I have gained much knowledge for ministry from individuals apart from any formal academic setting. A businessman who is not only my friend but also my mentor has taught me about business, labor relations, and perhaps most important of all, about faith. From month to month he has not known what the income would be from his business, but he has learned to walk by faith that God would care for him. Another friend, an attorney, has sent me books that I'd not normally read, introduced me to leaders from different professions I'd otherwise never meet, and gently prodded me to ponder beyond my conditioned responses to life's issues. Others have ministered to me in similar ways— my wife, my children, students, church members, co-workers, friends, and acquaintances—each with knowledge to share and each willing to take time to share with me.

Some of my most helpful knowledge from individuals came when I left the classroom for the pastorate. I discovered that I was woefully ignorant in many areas of knowledge necessary to be an effective pastor. Fortunately the church was filled with outstanding Christians, persons from whom I could learn a great deal. I spent hours with these people learning as much as I could. From businessmen and administrators I studied management and administration; from bankers and financiers I studied money management and budgeting; from wise deacons I studied human relations and motivation.

Members of our church staff also became my teachers. From our business administrator I learned about stewardship and financial planning. From our minister of education I learned about the art of human relations. From our associate pastor, a retired chaplain, I gathered a wealth of knowledge about pastoral ministry and care. The list is practically endless—I learned the benefit of seeking out individuals and learning from them.

Informal Groups

Jesus apparently enjoyed the small-group method of teaching. Gathering a dozen disciples around him, he spent three intensive years imparting knowledge to them. Although he taught in formal ways to large crowds, he seemed to major on these twelve.

The small-group approach of Jesus was informal. Much of the communication of knowledge took place while the group was eating a meal, walking on a journey, attending a party, or sailing across the Sea of Galilee. There were no books, desks, or usual trappings of learning, simply a group of people learning from a leader and from one another.

Informal groups remain one of the best ways for Christian ministers to acquire knowledge. Some such groups have an informal organization, such as one that meets on a regular basis to discuss preassigned subjects. Others have no agenda; compatible individuals simply get together and share. Groups can be formed around an outstanding Christian leader, one with much to share regarding ministry.

Such informal groups can meet practically anywhere—in churches, homes, restaurants, offices. The times of meeting also can vary—for breakfast, at lunch, in the evening, on weekends. How often they meet is up to the group—weekly or monthly, regularly or irregularly. The place, time, and frequency is not nearly as important as the commitment to learn.

Conferences and Classes

Conferences and classes are in a sense small groups, but they are more formal and structured. There are literally hundreds of such conferences and classes to help people prepare for Christian ministry. Some of these are built around occupational interests, such as pastoring, counseling, writing, teaching, or administrating. Others are formulated according to one's place of service—groups of deacons, Sunday School teachers, outreach and evangelism leaders, or lay preachers. Still others are devoted to subjects such as Old Testament studies, New Testament studies, theology, church history, missions, or evangelism. Quite a number are directed toward special interests, such as how to share your faith, how to minister while on the job, or how to influence political structures for righteousness.

Some of the best classes and conferences can be found in churches. Sunday School classes are often sources for excellent knowledge about the Bible and the Christian life. Church training and mission study groups afford opportunities to acquire knowledge related to Christian ministry. Many churches have special conferences throughout the year that offer the opportunity to gain a constantly increasing amount of knowledge for ministry.

Denominational conferences are also sources for information. By reading denominational publications you can keep abreast of the conferences and classes being offered.

Special interest groups also sponsor conferences for Christians on subjects such as world hunger, church-state relations, evangelism, and missions. Normally these are advertised in Christian periodicals and by direct mail.

Classes and conferences are also available at Christian colleges and universities, conference centers, and camps. Most of these print schedules of their offerings on an annual basis and are more than happy to share them with those who ask. Some of these classes are available for an extended period at night or on weekends. Others are concentrated into a few days or perhaps a single weekend. Conference centers and camps usually offer week-long packages including lodging, meals, and classes for a very reasonable price.

With such a wide-scale offering of learning opportunities at low cost there is no excuse for the Christian minister to lack knowledge. Even if formal education is not possible, a person can obtain vast knowledge through the many learning opportunities made available by churches, denominations, schools, and other organizations.

Special Learning Centers

A number of specialized centers and institutes are available to the Christian minister. Some of these offer brief meetings, often highly individualized, such as interviews or personal conferences. Other sessions may last a week or more and involve research, guided study, testing, or conferences. Still others may be more extended, involving a year or more of specialized study. What makes this type of resource different from the conferences and classes discussed in the preceding section is that these centers and institutes offer certain learning opportunities at one location on a more-or-less continuous basis.

Some of the most helpful specialized resources are career development centers. Through a series of extensive tests administered over a number of hours, even days, a person can gain knowledge about himself. Some of the evaluation instruments are directed toward aptitude and talent, others toward likes and dislikes, and still others toward personality traits and profiles. No reputable evaluation center will tell you what to do with your life, but the staff will provide helpful counsel on many decisions related to ministry. Some of the best testing centers are operated by Christian individuals and institutions such as denominational agencies, colleges and universities, and counseling centers.

Other institutes and centers specialize in various subjects. These may stand alone or be a part of a larger institution, such as a hospital or college. Many hospitals, for example, offer training programs in counseling and clinical pastoral education. A number of colleges and seminaries have institutes for such subjects as church growth, preaching, Christianity and the arts, church and society, and Christian ethics.

Another type resource offers more setting than content. Scattered throughout the world are retreat centers for persons serious about learning. Although some provide conferences or classes, many afford only a quiet place to concentrate on learning. Many of these are open both to groups and to individuals.

How does one go about locating these special resources? Because no comprehensive list exists, you will need to ferret them out and make contact for further information. Consult experienced pastors, college and seminary teachers, denominational workers, and ministry specialists. With some effort you will accumulate a list of available specialized resources.

Written Materials

Books, periodicals, articles, pamphlets, computer printouts, tracts, correspondence courses, and programmed learning manuals are some of the more common forms of printed materials available to assist the Christian minister in gaining knowledge. Two major problems relate to using written material; first, so much of it exists that it is difficult to know what to use; and second, it is generally expensive. But there is no way adequately to prepare for ministry apart from using such material.

Some material ought to be purchased as part of the tools of the minister's trade: a good study Bible, several different translations of the Scripture, a Bible dictionary, a concordance, a topical Bible, and commentaries. Most persons will also want a few books in each of the major areas of knowledge related to Christian ministry as well as a number in their own special area of ministry.

Subscribing to periodicals and journals related to ministry exposes one to a wealth of knowledge. In addition, newspapers and news magazines keep one informed about current events and ministry needs. Specialized articles, pamphlets, and tracts are also helpful; many of these are free, made available by churches.

Once I thought I needed to buy all the books and periodicals I use, but I now doubt the wisdom of that. Certainly some must be bought, but there are other less expensive sources, such as libraries. If you buy, attempt to find used items by searching used book stores and ads in the newspaper. When purchasing new items look for sales in bookstores, shop for prices, and, when possible, order from discount houses.

Printed material is available to the minister in libraries. Most communities have a public library. In addition, schools, colleges, and universities have libraries whose holdings are usually open to the public on an application basis. Libraries not only have books and periodicals; they also often have a good collection of articles and pamphlets. The librarian will be happy to help you locate whatever you need. If a library does not have the item you want, it is often available through interlibrary loan. Many churches now have libraries, and larger churches may have more holdings related to ministry than the public library.

Audiovisuals and Other Learning Aids

Once books were the primary resource for gaining knowledge. That is no longer true. A wide variety of material is available to help in the process of acquiring knowledge. Tapes, cassettes, records, video-cassettes, movies, and computer programs all are used to present information on ministry.

Some of the material is relatively simple to use—a cassette on a subject of interest, for example. Other materials is more complex—a programmed learning manual with accompanying audiocassettes or videocassettes. Computer programs on ministry will likely become more and more available.

One of the benefits of audiocassettes is that they can be played as you do other things, such as travel in a car, work in the yard, or exercise. They can also be shared with friends and used in group study. Some churches loan cassettes on a wide variety of subjects.

Television programs providing knowledge useful for ministry are available. Educational channels, cable, and regular network programming all provide helpful information for the discriminating viewer.

Schools

The most traditional resources for learning are schools. Schools combine practically all of the other resources previously mentioned into one organized package. If possible a Christian minister should spend some time in a school program either in classes or through correspondence courses. The person going into a so-called religious vocation should definitely pursue studies in a school.

A variety of schools is available. Some, such as colleges and universities, provide general education with opportunities to specialize in various areas of Christian ministry. A college education is foundational for practically all other learning. Specialty schools are also available for Christian ministers—Bible colleges, Bible institutes, theological seminaries, and graduate schools in religion. Some of these are operated by denominations and others by various religious groups. They differ widely in their offerings, theological perspective, and quality of instruction. Most offer at least some classes at extension centers; some provide correspondence courses.

How should one go about selecting a school? Although this is an individual matter and depends largely upon background, circumstances, and location, I would consider at least the following: Is the school accredited? Is the school church-centered? Is the school biblically based, Christ centered, and mission minded?

How do you go about determining what a school is really like? Visit the school if possible, sitting in classes, talking with students, visiting with professors. Study the school's catalog, carefully noting course descriptions, purpose statements, and student activities. Note how well graduates are performing in ministry. Talk with mature Christians you respect and see what their evaluation of the school is. Pray about the choice, seeking God's guidance as to what you should do.

When you enter a school, whether it is for a short course or for a degree, full-time or part-time, on campus or through correspondence, bring to it all of the right attitudes for learning. Take advantage of all the school has to offer. Maintain a good balance between study, family, work, and church; many students become unbalanced, frequently neglecting one of the important ingredients in life. You'll be no busier in school than at other times in life; if you cannot maintain wholeness there, you'll not likely maintain it anywhere.

Continuing Education

No one should ever stop learning. A degree from a school is primarily a license to learn, not a certificate of completion. Most high schools, colleges, and seminaries offer excellent courses in continuing education for graduates and others. Some courses, open for auditors or part-time students, are on campus. Other study is available through a guided reading program with books borrowed from the library, sometimes by mail.

An increasing number of schools offer certificates for earning the continuing education units. Some even have diplomas for fulfilling a program of study. For those in church-related occupations, the doctor of ministry degree is a popular approach to continuing education; available only to those who have basic theological training and experience in ministry, it combines both academic study and practical experience on a graduate level. Many persons in doctor of ministry programs are experienced ministers, some in mid-life, seeking retooling, updating, and motivating.

Continuing education programs are available to practically anyone. You can find out what is available from high schools, colleges, and seminaries in your area by calling or writing for a brochure or catalog. The cost is usually minimal, and the rewards are great. People enjoy not only the learning but also the opportunity to relate to other persons with similar commitments.

Obviously the resources for gaining knowledge are many. Basic to all learning is our primary Resource—God Himself, the One behind all truth. In his grace he has provided many resources for our benefit—individuals, informal groups, conferences and classes, special learning centers, written materials, audiovisuals and other learning aids, schools, and continuing education, most of which are available through church and denominational programs. By utilizing them, we will grow in knowledge and wisdom. As Mrs. Vester T. Hughes, an octogenarian Baptist leader, said to me one day after surveying Baptist educational resources, "There is absolutely no excuse for any Christian to be ignorant."

PART III
Skills for Ministry

While our family was living in New York City on Manhattan Island, we enjoyed the many benefits of America's most populous metropolitan area. Having grown up in a small town in the Southwest, I was bewildered by the array of world famous places and events only minutes away from our apartment on Riverside Drive overlooking the Hudson River. A one-block walk took us to the subway station. From there the trains carried us under the busy city streets to a hundred delightful destinations.

One day we ventured to Carnegie Hall for a concert by a famous Texas pianist. With seats at the front and in the center, almost on the stage, we were able to observe every move and expression of the famous performer. When the tall, slender, young man began to play, his body was tense and his face furrowed with concentration; but as the concert progressed his face revealed sheer ecstacy. When he finished, the concertgoers erupted in a roar of applause and cheering. Carnegie Hall was alive with joy.

On the way home I reflected on the relationship of joy, discipline, and freedom. Being a piano dropout myself, I had an inkling of how much work, how many hours of practice, how great a sacrifice went into his ability to play the way he did. He was free to play in such fashion only because he had paid the price of years of disciplined practice. And his joy and that of the audience were possible only because of that freedom. A basic principle began to form in my mind: There is no joy without the freedom to do a task well; there is no freedom to do a task well without highly developed skills; there are no skills developed without discipline. Discipline develops skills that lead to freedom that makes joy possible.

Since that time I have observed the principle in action over and over again. Allison, our youngest daughter, took homemaking as a sophomore in high school, a course which included sewing. When she first began to sew, the experience was total frustration. But she stuck with it. Gradually she acquired the skills that gave her the freedom to make beautiful things with thread and cloth. I'll forever remember the joy on her face as she showed me the first dress she had made.

Meredith, our older daughter, when first attempting to ski fell again and again in the snow. It was no fun. But she continued to try. Soon she acquired the skills for skiing and then the freedom to ski well. I recall the joy on her face as she swished to a perfect stop following a skilled run down the side of the mountain.

We are not free to know the joy of ministry until we have paid the price to acquire the skills for ministry. But there is not enough time in life to acquire skills for all ministries. Since we can't do everything, we must be selective. That calls for following God's direction to the ministries that are to be ours and then busying ourselves with the task of developing the needed skills to free us to perform these ministries.

The following seven steps will help us acquire the skills called for. Each is enhanced by an attitude of humility and a desire to develop the skills necessary for ministry. No one can force these on us; we must voluntarily follow them.

Instruction through a book, a lecture, or a film is the first step in acquiring a ministry skill. Although such instruction will not in itself develop a skill, it will provide an overview of what we can expect. Reading a book about preaching, for example, will not in itself enable a person to preach, but it will help him be aware of the elements in preaching.

Observation is important in skill development for at least two reasons. First, by observing someone perform the skill we gain confidence—that person did it and so can I—and second, we are provided a model of excellence. It is important to select carefully those we observe because their performance will affect our action.

Supervision, a third step, is closely linked with observation. Without a skilled supervisor we will likely pick up bad habits from observing others, even the best. Most of us tend to imitate the worst features in others rather than the best. A supervisor, a coach, a gifted teacher will monitor our development, help us correct bad habits, and instill in us proper procedure. Keep in mind that a person who is able to do a task well may not be able to teach another how to do it well. There is a difference in performance and supervision. Supervision in itself is a skill. A top-notch supervisor knows how to guide others in skill development. Find the best person available in the area you want to develop and put yourself under his supervision. The following four steps are best carried out under such skilled supervision.

Repetition or practice is a boring, if not painful, part of skill development. But for good performance it is necessary to go over and over an activity until it becomes second nature. Concentration, discipline, persistence, perseverance—all these and more are necessary for productive practice.

Correction of our performance is carried out under the direction of the supervisor. By spotting what we are doing wrong and by pointing it out to us, the supervisor provides a valuable service. Otherwise the improper method would be so engrained in us that it would be difficult to eliminate later. A perfectionistic attitude, an impatient spirit, an unwillingness to accept criticism—all these will short circuit the learning process. Accept correction gracefully.

Action with our acquired skills day by day helps us to keep the skills sharp. We lose what we don't use. When we get to the action stage, we begin to experience some of the joy of service, some of the fruit of the discipline of skill development. True, we may have a long way to go before we are really effective—but we are on the way. That in itself is a thrill.

Evaluation of our efforts by a supervisor or a more skilled minister is always helpful. If we are open to suggestions from others, if we show that we genuinely want to improve, there will be those to help. We should constantly ask ourselves: How am I doing? How can I improve? Have I picked up bad habits? In every field where skill is important periodic checkups are normal routine. A pilot's skills are frequently checked. A professional athlete undergoes evaluation after every game with suggestions made for improvement. An administrative team debriefs action to see how things could have been done better. If inspection and evaluation are important in secular activity, how much more important they are in the work of ministry.

Remember, there is no joy in ministry without the freedom to minister well. There is no freedom to minister well without developed skills. There are no well-developed skills without paying the price to acquire them through a disciplined procedure. May we all know the joy of Christian ministry because we have paid the price to be free to serve skillfully.

The following three chapters discuss the skills necessary for ministry. The skills are divided into three groups: those needed for life in general, those distinctive for the Christian life, and those essential for basic ministry. These discussions do not deal with specific ministry tasks or jobs, such as pastoring or teaching. Nor do the chapters deal with highly technical, specialized skills which may be used in ministry, such as counseling, music, psychiatry, surgery, or translating languages. Instead, the skills are those applicable to any Christian minister in any position.

7
Skills for Life

Although the knowledge required for different ministries may vary, the basic skills remain the same. Once these skills are developed, a person can function in many different capacities. The basic skills discussed in this chapter are necessary for daily living as well as practically any ministry effort.

Thinking

God obviously expects us to think as clearly as possible. He has given us a magnificent instrument to use in thought, the brain. In his Word, he has highlighted the importance of reason even while warning us of its limitations (Isa. 1:18; Matt. 22:37; Jas. 1:5).

The processes of thought are awesomely intricate. No one knows exactly how the brain works. We do know that different people have various degrees of ability in the thought processes required for the many phases of human activity. Some are quite gifted in abstract reasoning. Others are highly capable in technical areas. Only a few people seem proficient in all types of thought processes. We can't all be geniuses or masters of all fields of knowledge, but we all can develop the skill of thought.

Practice concentration. Discipline yourself to stay with a subject, question, or issue, not letting your mind wander. Daydreaming, allowing the slightest distraction to interrupt a thought process, permitting thoughts to skip from subject to subject with no direction or positive result—these are all enemies of sound thinking. They can best be corrected by practicing concentration.

Study and follow the rules of logic. Courses of study in logic or the so-called scientific method will help. To be sure, some problems may defy logic, but logical thought is an asset to ministry. It assists us in making good decisions, using time efficiently, and helping persons with problems.

Exercise your brain. Stretch its capacity. Those who study the function of the brain estimate that we use only a tiny fraction of its capacity. They also have determined that through mental exercise we can expand that capacity and increase our brain's ability to function. Engage in reflective thought, brainstorming, and "thinking outside the lines." Such exercise helps to jolt us out of a rut of habitual or routine thought. Certainly the brain needs some time to rest, but most of us rest our brains too much. When you are tempted to put your mind into neutral, engage your thought gears and shape up the thinking processes.

Through studying and learning we gain the tools for adequate, clear thinking. The entire preceding part of this book dealt with the importance of knowledge acquisition. Acquiring knowledge is in itself a skill, a lifelong task. If one does not develop the skill of studying and learning, he will be crippled in whatever ministry he undertakes (2 Tim. 2:15). Indeed, thinking, learning, and studying are all intermingled: thinking is part of the learning process, and through learning we gain resources for sound thought.

While I was teaching at a seminary, a new professor joined our faculty. From Holland, he brought with him the European approach to the classroom. In contrast to the popular American method of lecture mixed with a large amount of dialogue between professor and student, the European method is a more formal lecture by the professor with few interruptions expected from the student. In one of this professor's first classroom sessions, halfway through the lecture, a student frantically waved his hand for attention, interrupted the professor's lecture, and blurted out, "On that point, I think. . . . " In a Dutch accent the professor interjected, "Vait! Vait! You don't know enough to think yet. Vait until de end of de semester, then you'll know enough to think." Many of us need to study and learn in order to be able to think more effectively.

Planning

Planning is a big part of life. Planning a trip, a business enterprise, a ministry effort, a church program, or a life are all important. Unfortunately, some people do little planning or plan haphazardly. Things go better with good planning (Luke 14:28). In brief, planning is determining an orderly process of getting from where we are to where we want to be. As such, there are certain questions that must be answered in a planning process.

"Where do we want to go?" is the first question. What is our goal? What is our objective? What do we want to achieve? The ability to state clearly, simply, and concisely the answers to questions such as these is vital to good planning, while muddled thinking about a goal is one of the worst obstacles. A goal ought to be stated in terms of results, not procedure, and of accomplishment, not activity.

"How do we accomplish the goal?" is the second basic question. The answer calls for a strategy. The best strategies are usually simple, consisting of only the major matters needed to achieve the goal. They are often misleading in brevity and simplicity because the many options that have been considered and discarded are not evident.

"What are the priorities?" is the third basic question. Clearly we cannot do everything we would like to do or feel we need to do. The careful development of strategy often helps to set priorities, limiting what we will undertake. But even when this is done it is usually obvious that we cannot undertake even all of the priority items at one time. We must determine which ones are most important. Sometimes a logical sequence is evident. When it is not, leaders must act on what they feel is best.

"What is needed to implement the strategy?" is the fourth basic question. The answer involves what are sometimes called tactics. These are the resources and programs needed to carry out the strategy which has been adopted. Answering this question raises a number of others such as "Where do we get these items?" "How do we pay for them?" and "How do we provide the training for the personnel?"

"How shall we adjust what we are doing?" is a continuing question in the process of planning. Once we begin to act on a plan its effectiveness can be measured and its consequences noted, enabling us to see what we should do for improvement. A well-developed plan should not be quickly abandoned; it may take awhile for it to begin to work. On the other hand, a stubborn refusal to adjust could cause us to stay with a plan which is obviously in need of correction or rejection.

Organizing and Managing

Nothing much is accomplished apart from good organization. God obviously thinks organization is important. A casual observation of the universe indicates the order which is there. An examination of our own bodies reveals the value God places on organization; without the various structures and systems of our body we would be unable to function. It is no accident that the Scriptures use the human body to illustrate the nature of a church. Churches also must be well organized if they are to minister effectively.

Once a plan is developed, the next step is to organize to carry it out. Some people bog down in trying to come up with the perfect organization to implement the plan. Likely a number of different organizational approaches would work. There simply may not be any one best way to do things.

Some also want to wait to act until they have a perfect organization, but there is no such thing as a perfect organization. Organizations are made up of persons, and persons are finite and sinful. Furthermore, we never know exactly how an organizational structure will function until we use it. Only by seeing an organization in action can we determine what needs to be done to make it work better. If inventors had waited to fly until they could make a jet airplane, we would never have flown. Someone who is critical because an organizational structure functions imperfectly just does not understand the nature of planning and organizing.

One of the chief dangers of organization is that it will become an end in itself. An organization without a purpose beyond itself has no reason to exist. Effectiveness in achieving a goal, not merely efficiency, is the purpose of organization and management.

The primary skill in management is self-management. In a sense, we cannot manage time, facilities, or other resources. We can only manage persons who use time, facilities, and other resources. And the person we are most responsible for managing is ourself. Time management is really management of self to utilize time effectively. Money management is really the management of oneself to utilize financial resources effectively. Indeed, there are important skills and techniques for organizing and managing large structures, but the most important skill is that of organizing and managing oneself.

Cooperating

To use an analogy from the sports world, Christian ministry is neither a spectator sport nor an individual sport. It is a team sport. We can't minister while sitting in the stands and watching others in action. Neither can we minister effectively by trying to go it alone. Of course, there are solo ministry efforts, but effectiveness in serving others calls for working together. That is one of the reasons why God gave us churches. Working together in the body of Christ we have the capacity of meeting a vast array of human need.

The Bible's illustration of the church as the body of Christ highlights the importance of cooperation (1 Cor. 12:14-27). As Paul indicated, all members of the body are important. The foot cannot see where to go without the eye. The eye cannot go where it sees without the foot. We each need one another. When one of us fails to function in ministry, the entire body malfunctions. As a result, someone's need goes unmet.

Cooperation is indeed a skill, one which can be developed. It is primarily a skill of relating to and working with others, recognizing the importance of their gifts and talents. It also involves leading and following. None of us is totally a leader or totally a follower. Each of us is expected to do a bit of both.

The skill of relating harmoniously to others requires constant attention. Even the best of us tends to be selfish and self-seeking. We need the help of God to be effective in our relationships with others.

Decision Making

One of the primary skills of life is that of decision making. Life in one sense is a string of decisions, each one affecting those which follow. We are the product of the decisions we have made, the sum of our choices. Effectiveness in life and ministry is closely related to the ability to make decisions and solve problems.

Christians differ widely in their ability to handle decisions. Some panic in the face of multiple choices. Others calmly apply the skills of decision making and move on to the next issue.

Decision making is related to practically every other skill. Thinking, learning, planning, relating, listening—all these are in a sense a part of decision making. Decision making is closely related to life-style, character, and personality. We do not make decisions in a vacuum but rather out of the context of our values and loyalties; for the Christian, decision making is really finding the will of God.

Decisions should be faced squarely and acted on as quickly as possible. To delay is often to have the decision made for us. Of course, we can act too hastily, but generally the problem is procrastination and overanalysis largely due to our fear of being unpopular or wrong. We will not always make popular decisions. We cannot always be right. In baseball if a player gets a hit one-third of the times at bat he's rated excellent. In business if an executive makes the right decision half the time he's considered effective. Why should we feel we must always be right? If we wait until we feel absolutely certain the decision is right, we will seldom act.

Furthermore, it is difficult to know until after a decision has been made whether it is right or not. A decision may be well made and yet prove to be wrong because of circumstances beyond the control of the decision maker. This feature of decision making makes grace especially important to the believer. Because we will be wrong sometimes, we should be thankful for God's grace and forgiveness and learn to forgive ourselves.

Ability in decision making can be improved by study and practice. The steps to take in decision making are relatively few and clear: First, identify the problem or the objective to be reached. Second, gather as many facts as possible about the problem or issue. Third, state the options for dealing with the problem or issue. Fourth, evaluate the options in light of values, beliefs, and commitments, especially as revealed in Scripture. Fifth, reach a conclusion through both logical thinking and prayer. Sixth, tentatively act on the decision, monitoring how you feel about it; sometimes a hunch or intuition is helpful. Seventh, evaluate the decision, making whatever adjustments seem called for.

Communicating

Communicating decisions, plans, beliefs, information, and other matters is a highly important skill. The ability to communicate both in speaking and writing is absolutely essential to a teacher, politician, and preacher. Some specialized forms of ministry combine communication with other skills. Preaching and teaching, for example, combine studying, understanding the Bible, and communicating. But communicating is highly important for all of us. The best plan in the world is ineffective if it cannot be communicated. A meaningful truth does little good if it cannot be clearly shared.

How can communication skill be improved? First, become familiar with the various purposes of communication and fit what you communicate to the purpose. Do you want to inform? Inspire? Persuade? Motivate to action? If you want only to inform, then fact alone may be sufficient. But fact alone is seldom sufficient to inspire, persuade, or motivate.

Second, work on stating exactly what you want to communicate. Clear communication is based on clear thinking. It also helps to have a good command of language, which is improved by reading and thoughtful conversation.

Communication depends not only on clarity of thought but on organization, on arranging material so that the listener is carried from point to point without loss of a train of thought. Logical thinking is an aid in this aspect of communication. Outlining the subject matter in an orderly fashion also helps.

Effective communication requires that the listener keep on listening. You cannot communicate if someone will not listen. Keep the listener's attention by making what you say enjoyable or profitable, by using illustrations, clear organization, various emotional appeals, and by speaking enthusiastically.

Another factor in effective communication is understanding those with whom you are communicating. The very word *communication* implies give and take. If we communicate well with others, we will understand them—what they are interested in, what motivates them, what they are capable of learning.

Listening

Listening to others is vital to understanding them and communicating with them. Listening is a major skill in ministry. Careful listening lets us know why someone hurts and how we might help. Careless or indifferent listening damages the possibility for ministry.

Effective listening is not easy. How can we improve our listening skills? We can practice being attentive, concentrating on what a person is saying. We may be able to talk on the telephone, scribble notes, and listen to someone all at the same time, but what all that activity demonstrates is not brilliance but lack of interest. We should practice giving our full attention to the persons talking with us. We can discipline ourselves not to think ahead about what we are going to say in response but rather to concentrate on what is being said to us.

Listen to what a person is saying beyond mere words—in inflection, pauses, tone. Learn to listen with your eyes. Observe what a person does with head, hands, feet, and body during a conversation. Facial expressions and body language often communicate a great deal. The importance of listening with your eyes highlights the need for concentrating because you cannot do this and put your visual attention elsewhere.

Help the person to whom you are listening know you really are listening. This can be done by a nod, by facial expressions, by asking a question, or by summarizing what you think has been said.

Many persons in ministry find it helpful to make notes following a conversation. Usually it is best not to make such notes while the conversation is taking place because of possible distraction. If you do make notes it helps to say to the person, "Would you mind if I take a few notes? What you are saying is so important that I don't want to lose any of it." Writing a summary of the conversation not only provides a helpful record for reference, but it also improves listening skills. By forcing yourself to summarize you quickly become aware of how much you are really hearing and remembering and how much you are letting go past you.

The skills described in this chapter are important in all phases of life, but they are especially significant for the Christian minister. Developing these skills will enhance ministry, whatever form it takes. A weakness in any one of these results in a handicap to the person seeking to minister in Christ's name. It is definitely worth the price to be paid to develop the skills of thinking, planning, organizing and managing, cooperating, decision making, communicating, and listening.

8
Skills for the Christian Life

Paul, the great missionary apostle, writing from prison declared, "Rejoice in the Lord alway: and again I say, Rejoice!" (Phil. 4:4). Nothing about his circumstances indicated that Paul should be rejoicing. He was in a Roman prison—dark, damp, likely invaded by cold and infested with vermin. Some of the churches he had given his life to establish seemed about to disintegrate. His own death appeared close at hand. Yet, he knew joy, and he wanted those to whom he wrote to experience it also.

Paul possessed joy because he had thoroughly developed the skills for Christian living. He wanted those to whom he wrote in Philippi to have those same skills and to express that same joy. Why? Certainly because he loved them and wanted the best for them. But he also realized that they would be ineffective ministers to others unless they possessed joy.

The same is true today—we minister successfully to the degree we minister with joy. Telling someone of the love of God while looking as if we had just emerged from the Slough of Despond is no way to minister. Many would-be Christian ministers are ineffective because they lack the necessary skills to live the abundant Christian life. In addition to the skills required for living life in general, we also need to develop the skills for Christian living.

Understanding the Bible

Understanding the Bible is paramount for ministry. The Bible is God's word to us. "All scripture is given by inspiration of God, and is profitable for doctrine, for reproof, for correction, for instruction in righteousness:

That the man of God may be perfect, throughly furnished unto all good works" (2 Tim. 3:16-17). God has given us the Bible to help us in ministry. Without a knowledge of the Scripture we are ill-equipped for service.

The Bible tells us our purpose for ministry, the nature of ministry, and the method of ministry. It is simply impossible for us to know what we should about ministry apart from understanding the Bible. And understanding the Bible requires certain skills. The Holy Spirit will illumine the Word for us, but we work together with the Spirit in interpretation and understanding. And how do we develop the skill of Bible study?

First, approach the Bible with an attitude of reverence, a spirit of awe. The Bible is the Word of God. We should, therefore, want to know what God's Word says. Unless we really want to know what the Bible teaches, we will not pay the price to acquire the skill for adequate Bible study.

Pray for God's assistance in understanding his Word, especially for the guidance of the Holy Spirit. The One who inspired the writing of the Bible is our best source of help in interpreting the Bible.

Study the Bible itself, not just materials about the Bible. Learn to use the basic tools for Bible study—concordances, Bible dictionaries, topical Bibles. Gain a grasp of the organization of the Bible, the history of God's dealing with his people, the teachings about key doctrines, the biographies of primary persons, and the key Scriptures on various subjects. Memorize the books of the Bible and the chronology of key events in the story of the Bible.

Apply the principles of sound exegesis, the method of determining the meaning or teaching of a passage of Scripture. Among these are the following: Interpret a passage in its context. Take into consideration its type of literature, such as poetry, prose, drama, and its historical setting. Use passages with a clear meaning to help unlock the meaning of those that are more obscure. Study carefully the meaning of words and their grammatical relation to one another in a passage. Maintain the life and teachings of Jesus as the key to biblical interpretation.

With some effort you will become familiar with the Scriptures, comfortable in the use of the Bible. As you more and more enjoy the study of Scripture you will give more and more time to it. In so doing you will further equip your life not only for Christian growth but also for Christian ministry.

Praying

During a prayer seminar in a large church I was astounded at how many persons declared that they did not really know how to pray. They had been exhorted to pray, made to feel guilty because they did not pray, and even asked to pray—but no one had taught them how to pray. Many of these were older persons who had been Christians for many years.

The disciples must have felt much the same way. They said to Jesus, "Lord, teach us to pray" (Luke 11:1). We all need to know how to pray. Prayer is one of the basic skills of the Christian life. Through prayer we are helped to find God's direction for our lives, to discover God's enabling power, to minister to others through intercession, and to commune with God. Prayer is essential for Christian ministry.

In response to the disciples' plea, Jesus provided them a model prayer, not one simply to be memorized and repeated, but one to provide an outline for prayer (Luke 11:2-4). Jesus taught that prayer consists of at least four elements. First, adoration of and praise for God initiates prayer. Our thoughts are to be on God—his majesty, greatness, goodness, holiness, love, righteousness. We spend much of our time concentrating on ourselves; prayer is an opportunity to concentrate on God. From Jesus' model prayer it is clear that prayer is to be directed to God. Others may listen in, but it is to God we pray. We are to speak to God with an awareness of our relationship to others, praying "*Our* Father which art in Heaven" (Luke 11:2, author's italics).

Second, prayer is an act of submission: "Thy kingdom come. Thy will be done, as in heaven, so in earth" (Luke 11:2). Prayer helps get us in step with the will of God. There is little use seeking God's will in prayer if we are not going to follow it. Such a note of submission puts things in proper perspective: We are the creatures; he is the creator. We are weak; he is all powerful. We are finite; he is infinite.

Third, prayer consists of petition—for us and for others. We seek that which is necessary for life—daily bread. We seek forgiveness and God's assistance in forgiving others. We seek guidance and protection. All of this is for ourselves *and* for others; intercession is certainly part of prayer.

Fourth, confession is to be included in our prayer—confession of our sinfulness, weakness, and proneness to walk the way of the Evil One instead of the Holy One.

Many other things are taught about prayer in the Bible: how we are to pray, for whom we are to pray, the requirements for prayer, the place of persistence in prayer, the relation of prayer and purity. All of these can be gained from the study of the Scripture. Remember, prayer is a gift from God, but it is also a skill to be developed.

Meditating

Often I have felt the need to seek a quiet place and spend time meditating. Meditation is different from prayer. In prayer we often storm the battlements of heaven with our petitions and pleas, but in meditation we seek to cease all activity, including prayer. We simply become passively and reverently open to whatever God would share with us.

The Scriptures speak to our need for a quiet time. The psalmist declared, "The Lord is my shepherd; I shall not want. He maketh me to lie down in green pastures: he leadeth me beside the still waters. He restoreth my soul" (Ps. 23:1-3) and "Be still, and know that I am God" (Ps. 46:10a). The greatest victories of the heroes of the Bible were often preceded by a quiet time with God—Moses in the wilderness, Elijah at Cherith, David in the hills, Jesus in Gethsemane, Paul in Arabia.

The school of solitude can teach us much if we will only discipline ourselves to participate. And meditation indeed requires discipline. All around us life whirls at the furious pace of a tornado, sucking us into the tumult. Only discipline and determination will hold us still long enough to benefit from solitude in which we shut out the world and are shut in with God.

The benefits are priceless. Meditation enables us to come to grips with God's greatness and with our finiteness. It helps us to rekindle deep feelings, emotions, and convictions. It provides the stillness necessary for us to chart our course, to get God's direction for ministry.

Worshiping

Worship, closely related to Bible study, prayer, and meditation, is commanded in the Scriptures (Heb. 10:25). Worship is an opportunity, but it is also a responsibility. It is a means by which we gain understanding into the nature of God and of ourselves, but it is also a duty we owe God. Most of us testify that the more we come to know God through worship, the less worship seems to be duty and the more it seems to be spontaneous celebration of his presence.

The Bible makes clear that worship does not automatically occur because people gather in a particular place, such as a church, or assume a specific posture, such as kneeling, or are surrounded by certain symbols and events, such as stained glass windows, organ music, and robed choirs. These can be an aid to worship, but they do not guarantee that worship will take place. Worship is primarily a matter of the heart, of attitude. We worship when we participate with others in service to God. The word *worship* comes from an old English word *worthship*, meaning that God is worth the dedication to him of all that we are and of all that we possess.

Worship is both a private and a public matter. The great persons of the Bible are all pictured in acts of private worship—persons such as Daniel, Moses, Paul, John, and, of course, Jesus. The Bible also describes group or corporate worship—the wandering Hebrews in the desert, the Israelites in the Temple, the disciples on the mountain. Private worship incorporates Bible reading, prayer, and meditation. Corporate worship is similar but requires participation with a group.

Corporate worship normally includes a number of ingredients: the praise and adulation of God through prayer and music; submission to God in the form of confession and offerings; instruction concerning God through Scripture, hymn text, and sermon; and dedication to God in the time of decision and invitation. Ministry to others in the name of God is a result of true worship.

To benefit fully from the experience of worship, we must participate and concentrate. We need also to learn how to respond to the various symbols and aspects of worship, seeking to be open to whatever God reveals to us and calls forth from us in the worship.

Christians should also develop the skill of leading in worship. For pastors and others who lead formal worship services it is essential, but all Christians should know how at least to direct family- and small-group worship. Although some worship services may be celebrative happenings, most need planning. In New Testament times trouble apparently arose over lack of order in worship services, and Paul instructed, "Let all things be done decently and in order" (1 Cor. 14:40). Plan worship to focus attention on God, not on the worshipers, to praise, honor, and glorify him.

Trusting and Obeying

Trusting God is a skill to be developed as well as a gift to be received. We are saved by grace. The Bible is clear about that. "For by grace are ye saved through faith; and that not of yourselves: it is the gift of God: Not of works, lest any man should boast" (Eph. 2:8-9).

Indeed the trust that saves is a gift from God. Yet the Scriptures also indicate that God calls us to trust him, to believe in him in order to be relieved from anxiety and blessed with joy. Thus, in a sense, trust is a skill to be developed.

And how do we increase our ability to trust God? First, reflect on God's power and love, which are the bases of trust. Make this part of your expression of adoration and praise for God in prayer. Allow this to be a part of your Bible study.

Second, review the history of God's dealing with his people, with his Son, with his church, and with you. Times of meditation are opportunities for such a review, relishing the wonder of God's love and grace and of the fulfillment of his promises.

Third, always try to do what you believe he is leading you to do. In this way you will experience the faithfulness of God to keep his promises. Only those who act by faith in response to God's commands will come to experience the fullness of his joy. We learn to trust by trusting.

Knowing and following God's will is an essential skill in the Christian life. That calls for trusting and obeying (1 Sam. 15:22). Trusting in God leads to obedience. Obedience begins in trust.

The first step in knowing God's will is wanting to know it. That calls for believing God's way is best and that he will reveal his way to us. We understand that God does not reveal all of his will to us at once, but we trust he will give us further instruction as we need to know. He is not likely to reveal to us more than we are willing to do. Thus obedience leads to further direction.

Christians develop different skills for discerning God's will, but certain basic ingredients seem necessary: direction gained from the Bible and through prayer; insight received from others—mature Christians, friends in the faith, experienced counselors, the histories and testimonies of other people; assistance from within ourselves, from the conscience, spirit, and reason God has given us. By utilizing all of the resources God has provided, we can develop adequate skills for knowing his will. And then knowing, we practice obedience. As we obey, he opens up more and more of his purposes for our lives.

Effective ministry is based on a strong and mature Christian life. Such a life in Christ does not happen automatically but is the result of disciplined development of skills. Many Christian ministers are robbed of the joy which could be theirs if they would only pay the price to develop the necessary skills for abundant Christian living. If we are to be ready to minister, we must be continuously improving our skills for life in Christ. The Christian life is not an accomplishment; it is a process. No one has arrived; we are all on a journey. Step-by-step, we become more and more equipped to minister.

9
General Skills for Ministry

Jesus went about doing good, the Bible tells us. And we are to follow in his steps. Doing good for others calls for certain ministry skills, skills related not to a job but to a way of life. We are not really ready to minister effectively until we know how to evangelize, disciple, encourage, motivate, enable, comfort, and assist others.

People have many needs, and skills are required to meet those needs. One of the reasons why preparation for ministry is a process rather than an achievement is because ministry calls for an arsenal of skills that takes years to develop. Yet the only way to acquire skills is to develop them through use. That's why we prepare to minister by ministering.

Evangelizing

Jesus calls us to minister to total human need—physical, emotional, mental, and spiritual. Assisting a starving man by providing him food is a worthwhile ministry, certainly one that follows the example of Jesus. Yet without attempting to lead that person to a trusting relationship to God through Christ, we have ministered inadequately. We must be equipped to evangelize.

A person who trusts Christ has vast resources opened to him to meet life's challenges (Rom. 8:31-39; Eph. 1:15-23; 3:14-21). The unbeliever does not have those resources. Therefore, by evangelizing we not only equip people for eternal life but also for abundant life. The purpose of evangelizing is to help people respond to the gospel by believing in the Lord Jesus Christ and being saved.

Some persons think that evangelizing is a skill reserved for people who are pastors or evangelists, a special gift. They believe evangelism is carried out primarily through preaching and public appeals. Actually evangelizing is a skill which can be developed by any believer, and most evangelism takes place in private conversation, not in public meetings. Evangelizing is a skill that combines knowledge of the Bible and personal knowledge of Christ with an ability to communicate the good news about Jesus to others. Evangelism has been defined as one beggar telling another beggar where to find bread.

As a ministry skill, evangelizing is a step beyond witnessing. Witnessing basically is sharing what God has done for us through Christ; it is communicating a personal experience. In evangelizing, the minister needs to know not only what has happened to him personally but also what the Bible says about how persons are saved and how to communicate that message most skillfully. Although witnessing requires little or no preparation, evangelizing calls for training. Such training is readily available in evangelistic churches and denominations.

Most people either do not recognize their spiritual need for Christ as Savior or they are unwilling to admit it. Thus evangelizing often requires making people aware of a need rather than merely meeting a need. Furthermore, evangelizing sometimes gains less applause from the world in general than other forms of ministry. Many might commend a person for comforting a sorrowing woman, feeding a hungry child, or encouraging a depressed man, but be less sensitive to evangelizing an unsaved person. Therefore, the most basic ministry in many ways is the most difficult.

Discipling

Discipling is a ministry which goes hand in hand with evangelizing. As Christian ministers we have a responsibility to lead people not only to trust Christ as Savior but also to follow him as Lord. A favorite term in the New Testament for the followers of Christ is "disciple." This ought to give us a clue as to how important God regards this ministry skill.

Discipling others means helping them to grow to spiritual maturity. Discipling is really a collection of skills around a common purpose— helping others to become more like Christ. Discipling is a ministry for all believers, not just for those with a church-related job. The command of Jesus to his followers was not only to baptize, that is to evangelize, but also to make disciples (Matt. 28:18-20).

Although discipling can take place in a large gathering, it is usually more effective in a small group or in a one-to-one relationship. Discipling is both imparting knowledge and developing skills. It requires sharing with persons how they can grow in Christ through Bible study, prayer, worship, witness, service, and ministry. The goal of discipling is to help persons become mature enough in Christ to serve others.

As a skill, discipling requires training. In becoming a follower of Christ a person does not automatically acquire the skill of discipling. One becomes a discipler by having been a disciple. The ideal is for us both to be a disciple and a discipler. By placing ourselves under the careful supervision of a more mature Christian, we are aided in our growth in Christ and in our ability to disciple.

In a sense discipling is a preventive ministry. By helping others to grow toward maturity in Christ we equip them to deal with the issues and problems they will face. By being more mature in Christ they are better able to cope with grief, sorrow, fear, depression, and apathy. Discipling others equips them to minister to persons in need. In this way we multiply our own ministry. A person who ministers to others by evangelizing them adds members to the family of God one by one. But the person who ministers not only by evangelizing but also by discipling equips others to evangelize. In this way he helps grow the family of God by multiplication instead of by addition. We could experience a veritable population explosion in the family of God if every believer ministered not only by evangelizing but also by discipling.

Encouraging

While in college I received a call one day from a casual friend asking if we could get together for a visit. I agreed, pleased that he wanted to talk with me because he was the kind of person almost everyone admired—a campus political leader, handsome, well-dressed, suave, and popular. What he had to say shocked me. For hours he spoke of his discouragement and sense of failure. Despondent, dejected, afraid of the future, on the inside he was nothing like what he appeared on the outside. He desperately needed encouragement.

Since that encounter I have discovered many people need encouragement. Appearances are misleading. Successful businesspersons, professionals, politicians, actors, artists, teachers, students, farmers, and many others share a sense of discouragement with life. Wealth, education, position seem to be no defense against depression.

We need to be equipped to be an encourager. A readiness to minister means understanding the causes of discouragement, despondency, and depression. Sometimes the cause may be evident. A series of catastrophies or crises coupled with inadequate rest and food over a long period of time will give practically anyone the blues. But often the real cause of dejection is difficult to discern. It may be physical, such as a chemical malfunction in the body. It may be spiritual, such as a heavy sense of guilt. It may be emotional, such as an inordinate fear of the future or an unrealistic assessment of problems. Careful study of the causes of depression and despondency will equip us to encourage.

Sometimes we will encounter people with depression deeper than we are capable of handling. Then we need to refer them to more skilled ministers. For example, a person suffering from depression caused by physical malfunction needs a physician. Much of the time what is needed, however, is encouragement.

In ministering to a discouraged person, we need to avoid both the extreme of bubbly, effusive cheer and of gloom-and-doom pessimism. A calm display of confidence, an optimistic outlook, and an evident trust in God will help. Personal testimonies are often more useful than clinical discussions of depression or sermonic pep talks. When we are down it helps to hear someone say that he has been where we are, understands what we feel, and has come through the experience with God's help. Trust in God—in his love and in his power—is really the ultimate cure for most despondency.

Ministering to the discouraged calls for a knowledge of the many helpful Scriptures that deal with the problem. It also calls for a close relationship with Jesus who over and over again told his followers, "Don't be afraid. Fear not. Let not your heart be troubled."

A ministry of encouragement can take forms other than face-to-face conversation. Letters and notes frequently help. So do appropriate books and tracts. And, of course, intercessory prayer is a means of ministering to the fearful and fretting. The ministry of encouragement, in all of its forms, is both challenging and deeply satisfying.

Motivating

Motivating persons to do what is right and to refrain from what is wrong is no minor ministry. The irresponsible, lazy, procrastinating person hurts not only himself but others as well. Frequently the effect on himself is low self-esteem, guilt, and unstable relationships in marriage, work, and church. Because he fails to carry out his responsibilities, institutions and other social structures are crippled, and that means that people suffer. Someone must repair the damage he has caused. Many people need help in moving off dead center and doing their best. Motivating them to do so is an important skill.

Helping people to stop or abstain from doing what is wrong is also a vital ministry. Sin harms the sinner and those to whom he relates, whether it be of attitude such as greed, envy, hate, and lust or of action such as theft, adultery, murder, and drunkenness. The Bible indicates that ministers are to strive to motivate people to turn from their sins.

Effectively motivating others requires a thorough knowledge of why persons behave as they do. The Bible contains examples of various motivational techniques. Some appeals are positive, others negative. Some involve reward, others punishment. Biblical writers both rebuke and exhort. The Bible holds out both the promise of heaven and the threat of hell to motivate persons to faith in Christ. Appeals are also made to the highest motivations—to glorify God, to express love for God and others, to live up to the potential which God has given us.

The spiritual dimension is important in motivating. The more we know God the more we understand his love; the love of God constrains us to think and act according to his purposes (2 Cor. 5:14). Christ in us enables us to overcome lethargy, laziness, irresponsibility, and sinful thought and activity. We come to realize he has placed unlimited power at our disposal. We are able to say with Paul, "I can do all things through

Christ which strengtheneth me" (Phil. 4:13). And we are emboldened "because greater is he that is in you, than he that is in the world" (1 John 4:4).

Motivation ought not be manipulation. When one is manipulated he has no idea why he came to the position he holds. Manipulation brings no lasting results. Self-motivation is our goal. A person is not really helped until he has internalized the reasons for responsible behavior and made them part of his own value system.

Enabling

A significant ministry is performed by those who provide the structure, resources, and setting which enable others to utilize their gifts and training. Enabling is a ministry skill which is composed primarily of administrating and leading.

The skill of administrating can be developed by most persons, although some have more aptitude for it than others. Even though he may not spend full time administrating, every Christian ought to develop the skill because practically every kind of ministry calls for at least a little administration. Some will make it their primary ministry.

The skill of leading others to accomplishment is very important. It has to do with developing the ability to see the broad picture, establish priorities, take risks, and go out ahead of others. By leading we can help make good things happen. Leaders motivate others to achieve beyond what they would normally accomplish. They challenge people to move from being merely efficient to being effective, to reaching worthwhile objectives. Leaders help to shatter the shackles of timidity and fear. They help lift others above business-as-usual, replacing progress for useless activity.

Comforting

Seldom does a day go by that I do not encounter persons who need comforting—those in grief, suffering pain, distraught over divorce, disappointed in children or friends or co-workers, dying. Others are terrified by the world in which they live—crime, violence, war, economic uncertainty, political unrest, pollution, and a rapidly changing society. People long for peace, but there is no peace where terror and grief prevail.

If we are sensitive, we will be aware of the need for comfort on every hand. Some are quite effective in hiding their fear and distress, pain and sorrow, but when they sense someone cares, really cares, the masks are usually removed and the hurt shared. When that happens, the Christian minister should be equipped to comfort.

Comforting is a skill which requires understanding of the basic causes of human fear and the processes of grief. With an understanding of the nature of fear and grief we can more ably determine why a person is afraid and what stage of sorrow he is in and then minister effectively. At some stages of grief, for example, the best we can do is simply be present with an attitude of care and concern. No wise discourses, no pious remarks, no philosophical answers to hard questions are called for, just being there and caring is enough.

This aspect of the ministry of comfort was vividly illustrated one night in a group discussion at a church. People were sharing how the church met their needs in family life. One woman said, "I've lost two husbands. One by death, one by divorce. The pain was great in both cases. But I suffered most when I lost my husband by divorce because there was not only grief but also anger and guilt. When I lost my husband by death, friends from the church came in large numbers with food, words of comfort, promises of help. When I lost my husband by divorce, no one came. I was left alone to cope." Another member of the group blurted out, "But I wouldn't have known what to say." The woman replied, "You didn't know what to say when I lost my husband by death. But you were there. And simply being there was enough."

At other stages of grief, people need to express their feelings. At such a time we may best minister by listening. Later there may be opportunity for sharing, testimony, and even suggestions about attitude and action. Along the way thoughtful notes and helpful books are often a form of ministry, as is intercessory prayer.

Equipping people to deal with grief, fear, and death is an important ministry. All will face pain and death, trials and fearful circumstances. The best preparation for dealing with fear and sorrow is to become well acquainted with Jesus; "in all points tempted like as we are" (Heb. 4:15) and a "man of sorrows, and acquainted with grief" (Isa. 53:3), he understands. Similarly, we should help people become thoroughly familiar with the Bible, storing up portions of the Word of God in their memory for use when the painful days come.

Assisting

Presence and words are usually adequate for encouraging, motivating, and comforting. But often action is needed, and we must be "doers of the word, and not hearers only" (Jas. 1:22). John wrote, "Let us not love in word, neither in tongue; but in deed and in truth" (1 John 3:18). Frequently, people can't cope alone; they need assistance. Jesus told the story of the good Samaritan to illustrate that love was goodwill in action, meeting the needs of others (Luke 10:30-37).

The good Samaritan realized the man felled by the robbers needed help. A necessary ingredient in the ministry of assisting others is discerning what help is really needed. Physical assistance? Counseling? Financial aid? Transportation? Medical care?

Having sized up the need, action is called for, giving of our time and resources. If we don't have adequate time or resources to meet the need, then we ought to get help. But there are many needs we can meet on our own. In some instances our time and energy will be required, helping to repair a house, harvest a crop, or remove debris following a storm. Sometimes our expertise is called for—financial counseling, babysitting, welding, truck driving, well digging, whatever we know how to do that can meet a need. In other cases our money or physical resources will be required—assistance in paying bills, providing food for a hungry family, sharing clothing with the destitute.

In some circumstances we may need to teach and train persons so that they will be able to meet their own needs. A helping hand is usually better than a handout, although in crises a handout may be necessary. "Give a starving man a fish and he will be hungry again. Teach him how to fish and he will feed himself" is generally true.

Certain dangers are inherent in the ministry of assisting. Assisting people over and over again, doing for them what they ought to do for themselves, can lead them to become dependent. This is damaging to them. Our goal ought to be to assist others so that they will become as self-sufficient as possible, even able to assist people themselves.

Evangelizing, discipling, encouraging, motivating, enabling, comforting, and assisting are ministry skills that can be utilized by all Christians. Although training is needed to develop these skills, no lengthy, formal education process is required. Anyone can develop them. They can be used by persons in practically any setting, at any stage in life, with anyone in need. No one is adequately equipped to minister until he is developing these skills.

PART IV
Power for Ministry

The place looks like a graveyard for transportation vehicles—acres filled with old locomotives, railroad cars, automobiles, airplanes, and other transportation devices. Our family has spent hours climbing over the numerous vehicles, exploring the cockpits of airplanes and the engineer's booth of locomotives. Built as a museum of transportation, the place is interesting—but somehow depressing.

Why depressing? Because there sits the product of thousands of hours of human labor, the result of vast knowledge, the product of numerous highly-honed skills. Sitting there—that's the depressing part. Made to rush through the skies or roar over rails or zoom down highways, these engineering marvels sit immobile, rooted to the earth.

Skill and knowledge have made them capable, but lack of power renders them useless. They stand as mute symbols of the condition of many ministers. Equipped with skill and knowledge, they are capable of service. But without spiritual power, they are ineffective.

Failures in ministry stem more from spiritual immaturity and resulting character flaws than from inadequate knowledge or lack of skills. Christian maturity, spiritual vitality, and strength of character are absolutely essential for effective ministry. No one is really ready to minister until these are present.

The source of power for effective ministry is God, not ourselves. He implants power within us so that we do not ever have to feel impotent in the face of ministry need. And he equips us so that through faith and prayer we can tap into his power.

As we expand our spiritual maturity, we have more and more capacity for the power of God. Thus Christian growth and spiritual development are a vital part of readiness for ministry. Such growth is the product of grace and effort, the result of a gift from God and of our labor.

As we grow in Christ we become not only clear channels for God's power but also fit instruments for service in his name. God helps us to grow according to the model of a mature Christian minister set forth in the Bible. As we work with God life-style, character, and personality are shaped to equip us to be more and more accomplished in ministry.

10
Source

"If I were you, I wouldn't go to school. It will just take away your power."

That's the advice many young persons have received who have felt called into a lifetime of Christian ministry. Most of us have brushed aside such cautions, attributing them to ignorance. But the caution is not without merit. Many dedicated and zealous young persons have indeed gone to school for training in ministry only to return with polish but no power.

Actually the cause of the problem is not the education but the person's dependence upon education rather than upon God. As we become highly trained and well educated, we may begin to perceive ourselves as self-reliant, able to meet challenges with *our* skill and knowledge. The better approach is to obtain all the training and knowledge we can but also increase our dependence upon the source of all power, God.

The Source of All Power

God is the source of all power. As the Creator of all that exists, he infused the material world with power. The power of the sun, of gravity, of wind, and of tides are all expressions of God's power. Human beings do not create power; we only harness what God has provided. The force of a steamroller and the thrust of a jet engine are not human fabrications but manifestations of God's power.

So-called powerful people in business, politics, or education are not powerful in themselves. Businessmen may utilize the power and resources of the earth, such as in mining or construction, but the Bible tells us that it is God who gives us the power to make and get wealth

(Deut. 8:18). A politician may utilize the resources of human life, but it is God who created life. An educator may equip the brain for scientific discovery or aesthetic expression, but it is God who has equipped us with mental ability.

God's power is most brilliantly displayed in the spiritual realm. It is the power of God that redeems and transforms us, that translates us from death to life. As Paul indicated, the power of God is greater than we can comprehend: "Now unto him that is able to do exceedingly abundantly above all that we ask or think, according to the power that worketh in us" (Eph. 3:20). Anyone ministering to human need will be unwise to neglect the power of God. To do so would be as foolish as attempting to build a huge earthen dam with a child's sand bucket when a giant earth mover is available. Why rely on our puny human power when the mighty power of God is accessible to us in ministry?

The Potency of Grace

God's power is evident throughout the universe in many forms, but it relates most wonderfully to human life through his grace. Grace as an expression of God's power and love reaches out to us through his Son Jesus Christ. God's grace is powerful enough to give us spiritual life in place of spiritual death, to cancel the power and penalty of sin.

In his letter to the Ephesians Paul describes the power of God's grace. He prayed that the Ephesians might know "the exceeding greatness of his power to us-ward who believe, according to the working of his mighty power, Which he wrought in Christ, when he raised him from the dead, and set him at his own right hand in the heavenly places, Far above all principality, power, and might, and dominion, and every name that is named, not only in this world, but also in that which is to come" (Eph. 1:19-21). To the Ephesians he also declared, "But God, who is rich in mercy, for his great love wherewith he loved us, Even when we were dead in sins, hath quickened us together with Christ, (by grace ye are saved;) And hath raised us up together, and made us sit together in heavenly places in Christ Jesus" (Eph. 2:4-6).

A similar theme of the relationship of grace and power is found in

Paul's letter to the Romans. To them he wrote, "If God be for us, who can be against us? He that spared not his own Son, but delivered him up for us all, how shall he not with him also freely give us all things?" (Rom. 8:31-32). God in his grace chose to use his power to bring us salvation. He has also chosen to allow us to utilize his power in ministering to others. In a sense we become the channels of his power and grace.

The Enabling of Faith

The Bible teaches that we appropriate God's power through faith. The Scriptures declare, "For by grace are ye saved through faith; and that not of yourselves: it is the gift of God: Not of works, lest any man should boast" (Eph. 2:8-9). The entire process of salvation, grace through faith, is a gift of God, not the result of our work. Thus we have nothing to brag about.

Faith results in salvation, and it can also result in ministry. The letter to the Ephesians indicates that our ministry is in a sense the result of the interworking of grace, faith, and God's power: "For we are his workmanship, created in Christ Jesus unto good works, which God hath before ordained that we should walk in them" (Eph. 2:10).

Somehow our faith in God's power results in that power working in and through us. The ministry of Jesus demonstrates the close linkage of faith and the expression of God's power (for example, Luke 8:48-50). In Jesus' followers the power of God was also linked by faith with ministry to persons. Jesus taught his disciples about the relationship of faith and God's power. For example, he said, "Truly I say to you, if you have faith, and do not doubt, you shall not only do what was done to the fig tree, but even if you say to this mountain, 'Be taken up and cast into the sea,' it shall happen" (Matt. 21:21, NASB). Jesus also said, "All things are possible to him who believes" (Mark 9:23, NASB). Further, the enabling of faith is illustrated again and again in Hebrews 11 in those marvelous descriptions of people who lived by faith.

It is not that great faith generates great power. The power is from God, not our faith. Somehow as we trust in God's power rather than our own, his power works through us in ministry. As Paul declared, "But we had the sentence of death in ourselves, that we should not trust in ourselves, but in God which raiseth the dead" (2 Cor. 1:9).

Faith is not a means by which we manipulate God, directing his power this way and that. If such were the case, God would not be sovereign. To the contrary, the power that comes by faith is an evidence of God's sovereignty. On our own we are helpless in the face of overwhelming need, but through faith in God we can become his instruments to meet need.

The Relation of Power, Faith, and Prayer

How prayer works is a mystery, but that prayer does work is no mystery. Evidence throughout history and on every hand points to the close relationship of prayer and the power of God. It seems that prayer puts us in contact with God's power. The Scriptures record that those who were great powers for God knew the value of prayer and spiritual retreat.

Jesus spoke of the relationship of prayer, faith, and God's power. He declared, "Everything you ask in prayer, believing, you shall receive" (Matt. 21:22, NASB). In Mark it is recorded he taught, "I say to you, all things for which you pray and ask, believe that you have received them, and they shall be granted you" (Mark 11:24, NASB). In his own ministry, Jesus demonstrated the close relationship of prayer, faith, and God's power. Jesus spent much time in prayer. He prayed prior to his miracles, including the greatest miracle—his own death, burial, and resurrection. The apostles felt it important to give themselves continually to prayer and the ministry of the word (Acts 6:4).

Throughout history the same principle has held true—those who have ministered powerfully for God have been persons of prayer. Martin Luther declared, "I have so much business I cannot get on without spending three hours daily in prayer." John Wesley insisted, "God does nothing but in answer to prayer." He spent at least two hours a day in prayer. David Brainerd, the great missionary in Colonial America, records in his journals his devotion to prayer. Adoniram Judson endeavored to go aside by himself seven times a day in order to pray.

The message from the Bible and from history is clear: if we want to minister with power, we must spend time with God in prayer, believing that he will answer. Whatever keeps us from prayer—an overblown impression of our ability, busyness, sin, unbelief—should be sternly dealt with and prayer placed as a priority in life. Without the power of God we are not ready to minister. Without prayer we will know little of God's power.

The Power Within

We are not to think of the power of God as residing in some distant place but rather as immediate to us as our own persons. Why? Because the risen Christ and the Holy Spirit reside with the believer, each being an expression of the power of God.

The Bible teaches that the living Christ indwells the Christian. Paul wrote to the Galatians, "I am crucified with Christ: nevertheless I live; yet not I, but Christ liveth in me: and the life which I now live in the flesh I live by the faith of the Son of God, who loved me, and gave himself for me" (Gal. 2:20). The worldwide ministry of believers is based on the fact of Christ's power and his perpetual presence: "All power is given unto me in heaven and in earth. Go ye therefore, and teach all nations, baptizing them in the name of the Father, and of the Son, and of the Holy Ghost: Teaching them to observe all things whatsoever I have commanded you: *and, lo, I am with you alway, even unto the end of the world*" (Matt. 28:18-20, author's italics).

The Bible also indicates that when we are born again, God gifts us with his Holy Spirit. Jesus taught that the Holy Spirit brings power into our lives: "But ye shall receive power, after that the Holy Ghost is come upon you" (Acts 1:8).

Thus God does not send us out to minister in weakness but in strength. He literally goes with us as we minister. His power is available to us all of the time, present with us each moment. It is foolish to try to minister under our own power when the power of God is immediately available to us.

God is the source of all power, and most certainly the source of the power we need for ministry. Through his grace he makes that power available to us. By faith and prayer we are somehow able to utilize God's power in ministry. And the power is always as near as life itself, available to us as we minister. We are not ready to minister until we have come to trust in God's power, not our own; to utilize his power through faith and prayer; and to be aware of the indwelling Christ and Holy Spirit.

11
Means

God's power is limitless; he is omnipotent. Our use of God's power is limited. Our finite human natures can handle only so much of God's power; therefore, in some manner, God protects us from the full extent of his power. Yet often we do not utilize even the power God does make available to us.

Our life is a channel through which the power of God flows in ministry. If that channel is restricted, then in some ways God's power is not fully utilized. The flow of God's power through our lives is restricted in two ways primarily. Because of sin our channels are obstructed or closed. Because of lack of spiritual growth our channels do not expand but remain small, restricting the flow of God's power. We can clear a cluttered channel by confessing our sin and receiving the cleansing power of God's forgiveness. But expanding the channel is more difficult, requiring both time and effort.

The Importance of Spiritual Growth

Spiritual growth is called for over and over again in the Scriptures. According to the Bible God wants us to grow, to develop, to expand the capacity of our lives for spiritual power. We are not to remain immature, but we are to become mature: "Therefore leaving the elementary teaching about the Christ, let us press on to maturity, not laying again a foundation of repentance from dead works and of faith toward God" (Heb. 6:1, NASB). We are expected to grow: "Like newborn babes, long for the pure milk of the word, that by it you may grow in respect to salvation" (1 Pet. 2:2, NASB). "Grow in the grace and knowledge of our Lord and Savior Jesus Christ" (2 Pet. 3:18, NASB). Paul warns in his letter to the Corinthians that failure to grow, to remain babies in Christ, is to limit the joy and power of the Christian life (1 Cor. 3:1-3).

To the Ephesian Christians Paul stressed growth, using the body as an illustration (Eph. 4:11-16). In his letter to the Corinthians Paul emphasized the importance of growth, using three different illustrations of growth—the maturing of a person, the growth of a garden, the construction of a building. He wrote,

> And I, brethren, could not speak unto you as unto spiritual, but as unto carnal, even as unto babes in Christ. I have fed you with milk, and not with meat: for hitherto ye were not able to bear it, neither yet now are ye able . . . I have planted, Apollos watered; but God gave the increase. So then neither is he that planteth any thing, neither he that watereth; but God that giveth the increase. Now he that planteth and he that watereth are one: and every man shall receive his own reward according to his own labor. For we are labourers together with God: ye are God's husbandry, ye are God's building (1 Cor. 3:1-2,6-9).

While these three illustrations relate primarily to the growth of a church, they provide helpful insight into the means for individual Christian growth and thus the means for greater use of God's power in ministry.

The Growth of a Person

The Bible stresses that the Christian is to grow spiritually much as a body grows physically. The parallels are striking, indicating some of the necessary ingredients for Christian growth.

First, a person needs air in order to grow. Without breath there is no life. Similarly, the Christian needs the Spirit of God to live and to grow. The Bible teaches that God gives each Christian the indwelling of his Spirit. The believer's responsibility is to increase his awareness of and capacity for response to the Holy Spirit. "Be filled with the Spirit" (Eph. 5:18) is a command from God's Word.

Second, the body needs nourishment in order to grow. Babies eat and eat and grow and grow. Without nourishment there is no growth. And improper nourishment can stunt growth. It is important to eat the proper kinds of food. Likewise, we grow spiritually only as we take in spiritual nourishment. A regular, adequate, and balanced diet of God's Word is essential for growth.

Third, rest is necessary for growth. Babies sleep a great deal. All of us need rest. Without rest our bodies malfunction and sicken. In our spiritual growth we also need times of rest. A period of quiet meditation each day is a necessary ingredient for development in Christ. Carve time out of every day for a quiet-time appointment with God. At the appointed time, if at all possible, find a place of calm and quiet. Concentrate on the truth of God's Word, especially the promises he has made to take care of us, to comfort us, and to meet our needs. Contemplate why you can put absolute trust in God, how much you have to be thankful for, how many times God has expressed his love for you.

Fourth, exercise helps the body to grow. Muscles atrophy without exercise. Babies exercise almost constantly, pushing, grasping, rolling, squirming. And young children are busy at exercise in their play. Exercise is also essential for spiritual development. Believers whose main spiritual exercise is sitting and listening to a sermon or a Sunday School lesson will grow relatively little. More vigorous exercise is needed for healthy growth—the exercise of witness and ministry, of personal soul winning and Christian social action, of helping others in need and teaching people about the abundant life in Christ.

Fifth, cleansing the body and eliminating toxins from its system are essential to health and growth. Spiritual cleansing is vital for spiritual development. The Bible speaks of the need of God's people to be purged and cleansed of sin (Ps. 51; Col. 3:8). Even the most mature Christian falls into sin and needs cleansing. The Bible indicates that we need to confess our sin to God and to receive his cleansing and forgiveness (1 John 1:9-10). We cannot grow in Christ as we ought if we are laden down with unforgiven sin.

Sixth, love aids human development. Many experiments have been conducted which demonstrate that human beings do not develop physically, emotionally, or mentally as they ought without love from other people. In our Christian growth love is also vital. We need not only to be aware of and open to the love of God but also to experience the love, support, and encouragement of fellow believers. Because one of the ways God loves us is through other people, we need to be part of Christian groups. Only by being in a fellowship of people who share God's love can we really experience his love completely.

As you grow in Christ and increase your capacity for God's power and ministry, keep in mind how important it is that you utilize all the ingredients of growth illustrated in the development of a person from infancy to maturity. Each is important. Leave any one of them out, and you will stifle growth.

The Cultivation of a Garden

The Bible also compares the growth of a Christian to the cultivation of a garden or of a plant. This illustration of growth highlights the role of grace in growth. The finest gardener working with the best soil cannot bring life out of a seed. The potential for new life is put there by God. It is a given, a gift, an expression of grace. A seed exists to produce a plant and ultimately other seed. And so in the Christian life the potential for growth is a gift from God. In a sense, we cannot force ourselves to grow. God has already placed within us through his grace the potential for growth in Christ. In his letter to the Corinthians Paul twice makes the statement that God gives "the increase" (1 Cor. 3:7).

Although we cannot of ourselves bring forth life and growth—that's the prerogative of God—we can see that our lives are surrounded by those elements which contribute to growth. That's the way it is with the garden. The gardener cannot make life spring from the seed, but he can see that everything necessary is present for a new plant to be able to grow. We should endeavor to surround ourselves with everything necessary for good, solid growth.

A mixture of rich soil and adequate moisture provides the basis for a good garden. In the life of the believer, by keeping our lives open to the seed of God's Word and Spirit and moistened by the dews of his love, we provide the possibility for strong growth. By adding the nutrients of Christian friends, church fellowship, and a Christian atmosphere in work and recreation, we can further contribute to growth. In his parable of the sower, Jesus taught that we are responsible to be fertile soil for the

Word of God so that when the Word enters our lives it will take root and flourish there (Luke 8:4-15).

But fertile soil is not enough. Good soil produces weeds as well as desirable plants. For our Christian lives to grow adequately there must be elimination of the negative influences and destructive factors such as pessimism, doubt, fear, and materialism. Materialism, the love of things, is especially damaging to the Christian minister. Jesus warned, "The cares of this world, and the deceitfulness of riches, and the lusts of other things entering in, choke the word, and it becometh unfruitful" (Mark 4:19).

If plants are to prosper, they must be protected from more than weeds. Most plants suffer attacks by various outside forces such as insects, birds, animals, fungus, and extreme heat and cold. Farmers and gardeners deal with these attacks by endeavoring to develop plants which are resistant to such attacks and by protecting the plants with insecticides, fungicides, scarecrows, smudge pots, and other defenses.

Christians are also subject to attack from destructive forces. We need help to survive and grow just as a plant does. Plants have some built-in resistance to destructive outside forces, and so do we. The Scriptures indicate that "greater is he that is in you, than he that is in the world" (1 John 4:4). The Bible declares, "Resist the devil, and he will flee from you" (Jas. 4:7). We have at our disposal all the weapons necessary to resist "the wiles of the devil" (Eph. 6:10-20).

In the growth of a garden, when the soil is good and destructive forces are eliminated or controlled, the plants flourish. Then another step is necessary to insure the finest growth possible—pruning or thinning. And so in our Christian growth, we frequently must choose the best over the good. It is essential that we establish priorities and concentrate on what is absolutely vital. Sometimes we crowd our lives with so many good things that we actually stifle our growth in Christ. One of the keys to the apostle Paul's success in his own Christian growth is seen in his statement, "This *one* thing I do" (Phil. 3:13, author's italics). Solid growth calls for concentrating on a few things and doing them well.

The final step in growing a garden is to harvest and use the crop. After all, the purpose of gardening is not simply to grow plants but to produce food. And so it is with the maturing Christian. As we grow in Christ we begin to produce fruit. The mature Christian can minister to and help others in ways an immature Christian cannot. The process of growth brings ability which is not present in the seedling believer. We all feel better when we feel needed, wanted, and helpful. Thus by harvesting and using the fruit of Christian growth we bring not only joy to others but also to ourselves.

The Construction of a Building

The construction of a building is another illustration used in the Bible to help us understand the nature of and means to Christian growth. Paul speaks of himself as "a wise master builder" (1 Cor. 3:10). He seems to be referring to himself primarily as a builder of churches, but what he says also applies to the building of Christian lives.

The construction of a building calls for a plan. In Christian growth the same is required. For the Christian, the plan is essentially the will of God. God has a will for all of his children—for example, that they assemble together, worship, pray, witness, minister, and strive for justice. He also has a will and purpose for individuals, such as the work they are to do, the places they are to live, and the persons they are to marry. Building a Christian life requires a constant referral to the plan of God for one's life. God provides us resources to help us be aware of his will. Among these are prayer, the Bible, worship, reason, and the counsel of wise Christian friends.

Materials are also essential for a building. The better the quality of materials used the better the building constructed. In our growth in Christ we need to use the very best materials. We need to put into our lives that which is top quality. Shoddy materials will result in a shoddy life; excellent materials will produce an excellent life as we grow in Christ (1 Cor. 3:10-14).

A solid foundation is another essential for a good building. An uneven foundation, a weak foundation, an unlevel foundation—all spell disaster for a building. As we construct our lives in Christ, it is important that we make him the foundation (1 Cor. 3:11). In fact, the Scriptures speak of him not only as the foundation but also the cornerstone. Everything rests on Christ. If we try to build our Christian lives on our own abilities, intellectual capacity, intuitive feelings, or anything else, we are doomed to a less than desirable outcome.

Laying a solid foundation must be followed by constructing the walls, putting on the roof, and finishing the inside of the building. It is not enough to start. It is important to finish. Jesus warned those who would follow him that they must count the cost and be willing to keep at the task until it is complete. Readiness for ministry requires following through. Jesus told the parable of a builder who failed to count the cost, started a construction project, and left it unfinished—a monument to the failure to follow through (Luke 14:28-30). Unfortunately, many Christians are like that. They start off with great zeal to build a life in Christ but weary of the effort.

Work is necessary for a building. The body has within it the natural potential for growth; so does a plant. But a building does not. The materials, even the best of them, collected and laid out do not put themselves together into an edifice. Someone must take the materials, follow the plan, and work if the building is to become a reality. Such is also true in Christian growth. Developing the Christian life takes effort. It requires discipline and time. Too many people assume that becoming a Christian guarantees that they will grow to maturity in Christ. The Bible does not indicate this. Instead, the Scriptures emphasize work, study, discipline. When we have experienced these we are equipped to minister to others.

But work alone is not adequate to construct a solid building. Skilled labor is also necessary. The more skilled we become in Christian growth, the more we will enjoy our growing experiences. That shouldn't surprise us. The same principle holds true in practically everything we do.

God is the source of power for ministry. If we are to minister effectively, we must be able to utilize fully the power of God available to us. To do so requires that we increase our capacity for God's power by Christian growth through spiritual development. God expects us to grow and provides many illustrations in the Bible about what is required for that growth.

In addition, many aids are available all around us for assisting us in growth: mature Christians skilled in discipleship, small groups dedicated to helping the members develop Christian maturity, effective Sunday School classes, manuals and guidebooks for Christian growth, tapes and tracts on spiritual development, and, best of all, churches committed to helping their members grow in Christ. There is really no excuse not to grow in our faith.

12
Instrument of Ministry and Power

The Bible indicates a close relationship between purity and power, right living and effective ministering. It is "the effectual fervent prayer of a righteous man" that availeth much (Jas. 5:16). Isaiah warned the people of his day that because of their immorality God would not hear their prayers: "I will hide mine eyes from you: yea, when you make many prayers, I will not hear: your hands are full of blood" (Isa. 1:15).

Spiritual growth provides not only a clear channel but also a clean channel for God's power to work through us in ministry. A certain kind of person is described in the Bible as being a fit instrument in the hand of God to minister with power and effectiveness. The lives of great ministry leaders recorded in the Bible, such as Jesus, Paul, and Peter, provide insight through example. Many specific teachings relate to the kind of persons we are to be as God's ministers. Let's examine the qualities of that person from the viewpoint of life-style, character, and personality.

Life-style

The basic life-style of a Christian minister is related to the Trinity: Father, Son, and Holy Spirit. According to Scripture, a Christian minister is to be godly, Christlike, and Spirit-directed.

Godliness is to be a basic quality of a Christian minister. 1 Timothy states, "Godliness is profitable unto all things, having promise of the life that now is, and of that which is to come" (1 Tim. 4:8). The godly person is one whose life is totally committed to God, whose character is fashioned after the attributes of God. Jesus said, "Be ye therefore perfect, even as your Father which is in heaven is perfect" (Matt. 5:48).

The Bible does not call us to attempt to become like God in his essence—his omnipotence, omnipresence, and omniscience. That would be folly. But the Scriptures do point to the moral attributes of God as the standards for our lives. God is holy; we are to be holy. God is love; we are to love. God is righteous; we are to be righteous. God is just; we are to be just. God is merciful; we are to be merciful. Even though we know we cannot achieve God's perfection in these, we can move toward the goal set forth by his nature.

Christlike is another summary word indicating the life-style of a Christian minister. Paul wrote that we are to grow until we come to the measure of the stature of Christ himself. Of course, we will never reach absolute Christlikeness, but the goal should always be out before us, challenging us to become more like him. The encouragement to Christlikeness is seen in Jesus' frequent command, "Follow me." And New Testament writers stressed that we are to follow in his steps.

What does it mean to become like Jesus? Obviously we cannot become sinless as he was, or die for the sins of the world, or become a member of the Godhead. To be like Jesus means to live as much like he lived as is possible with our human limitations. Some characteristics of his life stand out, characteristics which become goals for us.

Obedience to the will of God, for example, was clearly evident in Jesus' life. He told his followers that he must do the will of the Father who sent him. Facing the awful agony of death by crucifixion to suffer for the sins of the world, he pled with the Father to let such a bitter cup pass away. Yet his final word was, "Nevertheless, not as I will, but as thou wilt" (Matt. 26:39). Obedience to the will of God should characterize the Christian minister.

Service also characterized Jesus' life. Jesus said that he had come to minister and to give his life a ransom for many (Matt. 20:28). He taught his disciples by word and deed that those who followed him must learn to be servants (Matt. 20:26-27). Greatness, he said, is measured in service (Mark 10:42-44). His entire life was spent ministering to the needs of others, symbolized by the washing of the disciples' feet at the Last Supper and climaxed by his death on the cross.

The cross-kind-of-life is a goal toward which we are to strive. The means of Jesus' death was a sign of servanthood as well as evidence of his absolute willingness to do the will of God. It showed that we should also be willing to suffer in order to help others. Suffering should come as no surprise to the Christian; it is a part of following Christ in service. Jesus told us, "If any man will come after me, let him deny himself, and take up his cross, and follow me" (Matt. 16:24).

Love was central in Jesus' life. Christ-kind-of-love is a goal toward which all of us are to grow. Jesus spoke often of love. He indicated that it was the love of God that sent the Son to be the Savior of the world (John 3:16). He told us that we are to love one another even as he loved us. He demonstrated love for all people and love for all of a person. Growth in Christ means we're to love, care for, and minister to all kinds of people everywhere.

Forgiveness was another basic quality of Jesus' life. His words from the cross "Father, forgive them; for they know not what they do" (Luke 23:34) stand as a summary of his life. He not only lived forgiveness, but he also taught forgiveness. Jesus indicated that we should seek forgiveness of those we have wronged (Matt. 5:23-24) as well as be willing to forgive those who have wronged us (Matt. 6:14-15; 18:21-35).

Simplicity characterized Jesus' life-style. He traveled light. His life was not cluttered by things. He had a clear-cut priority—to do the will of his Father in heaven. He was not concerned over a thousand and one things but only about carrying out his mission. His life had focus and unity. In contrast to Jesus, many Christian ministers lead fractured, fragmented lives, cluttered by too many things and too many activities. We are hindered by all the stuff than we must carry along with us. Some spend more time collecting, storing, repairing, and counting things than they do in ministry. We are unlike Jesus who said, "The Son of man hath not where to lay his head" (Luke 9:58). Ownership of things is not our problem. It is that things often own us. We have been victimized by materialism. And what is the answer? To follow Jesus who said, "Seek ye first the kingdom of God, and his righteousness; and all these things shall be added unto you" (Matt. 6:33).

Spirit-filled or Spirit-directed is another key quality in the minister's life-style. The effective ministers whose lives are recorded in the New Testament were Spirit-directed persons, such as Paul, Stephen, and Peter.

The Holy Spirit not only empowers us but guides us. Without the Spirit's help, the overwhelming amount of human need would confound and confuse us, but the Spirit directs us to those to whom we are to minister.

The Spirit also overcomes the obstacles and prejudices which might handicap our ministry. The Book of Acts records how the Holy Spirit led the early Christian ministers to overcome their prejudice and carry the gospel to Gentile and Jews alike. The Spirit is still working in our lives, overcoming prejudice and ill will, opening up avenues to ministry which otherwise would be closed.

The Holy Spirit is also the primary factor in the development of Christian character and personality. He helps replace the bad with the good, mold us in the image of Christ, and stretch us toward godliness.

Paul wrote to the Galatians about this ministry of the Spirit:

> Now the works of the flesh are manifest, which are these; adultery, fornication, uncleanness, lasciviousness, Idolatry, witchcraft, hatred, variance, emulations, wrath, strife, seditions, heresies, Envyings, murders, drunkenness, revellings, and such like: of the which I tell you before, as I have also told you in time past, that they which do such things shall not inherit the kingdom of God. But the fruit of the Spirit is love, joy, peace, longsuffering, gentleness, goodness, faith, Meekness, temperance: against such there is no law. And they that are Christ's have crucified the flesh with the affections and lusts. If we live in the Spirit, let us also walk in the Spirit. Let us not be desirous of vain glory, provoking one another, envying one another" (Gal. 5:19-26).

If we cooperate with him, the Holy Spirit will help us develop the character and personality needed for effective ministry. He will help us become fit instruments in God's service, able to tap the power of God to serve others. Let's look at some of the qualities he will develop in us as we work with him.

Character

A study of the Bible's teachings on attitudes and actions displeasing to God can be very fruitful, such as Exodus 20:1-17; Ephesians 4:17-22; 5:3-18; Colossians 3:5-10; and Titus 3:3. Even more constructive is to concentrate on God's Word concerning the qualities of character which please God, such as Psalm 1:1-3; 15; 24:1-6; Matthew 5:3-11; Romans 12:9-21; Philippians 4:8; Colossians 3:12 to 4:6.

The pages of the Bible are filled with insight on the character traits which please God and those that displease him. In passages describing the kind of person suitable for pastoral ministry, the Bible makes clear that vices detract from ministry while virtues enhance ministry (1 Tim. 3:2-6; Titus 1:7-9).

Of the character qualities of the mature Christian, several stand out as particularly important to the Christian minister. Being honest and just in both speech and action enhances a reputation for integrity, of great help in relating to people. A deep concern for justice compels us to right wrong, correct social injustice, and deal impartially with all kinds of persons. Responsibility, dedication, trustworthiness, commitment—these should characterize a minister.

Ministering to human hurt is often difficult and frustrating. Those who give up easily are ill qualified to minister. Often we will encounter resistance, misunderstanding, abuse, and even persecution. We need to be patient, persevering, and able to endure hardship, criticism, and persecution. A minister must be courageous, not buckling under to threats or hardship. These were some of the prime qualities that enabled Paul to carry out his ministry in spite of difficulty, danger, abuse, criticism, imprisonment, and the threat of death.

Pure in thought and action, a minister is equipped for service. Again and again the Scriptures call for purity. The psalmist asks, "Who shall stand in his holy place?" And the reply: "He that hath clean hands, and a pure heart" (Ps. 24:3-4). Paul enjoined the Philippians to think on those things that were pure (Phil. 4:8). And James wrote, "Draw nigh to God, and he will draw nigh to you. Cleanse your hands, ye sinners; and purify your hearts, ye double minded" (Jas. 4:8). Impure thought and action, filthy speech, obscene jokes, sexual immorality—all these undermine effectiveness in ministry.

The humble person, not the proud, is more likely to be the effective minister. He will be teachable, open to suggestions and criticisms. Being humble he will more likely follow the biblical injunction to be mutually submissive to one another (Eph. 5:21). James reminds us that "God resisteth the proud, but giveth grace unto the humble" (Jas. 4:6).

Disciplined persons also normally make more successful ministers than those who are not. Discipline applies to every part of our life. Paul realized the importance of disciplining his body, the temple of the Holy Ghost: "But I keep under my body, and bring it into subjection: lest that by any means, when I have preached to others, I myself should be a castaway" (1 Cor. 9:27).

Discipline in regard to what we eat and drink is especially stressed in Scripture. The writer of Proverbs declared, "For the drunkard and the glutton shall come to poverty" (Prov. 23:21). And Paul wrote to the Philippians, "(For many walk, of whom I have told you often, and now tell you even weeping, that they are the enemies of the cross of Christ: Whose end is destruction, whose God is their belly, and whose glory is in their shame, who mind earthly things)" (Phil. 3:18-19).

Likewise we are to discipline our emotions, our use of time, and our speech. A minister should be even-tempered, not given to temper tantrums and angry outbursts. He should be hard working, not lazy or slothful. He should speak praise and encouragement, not gossip and censure.

The Bible especially stresses the importance of controlling the tongue: "Let no corrupt communication proceed out of your mouth, but that which is good to the use of edifying, that it may minister grace unto the hearers" (Eph. 4:29). "Neither filthiness, nor foolish talking, nor jesting, which are not convenient: but rather giving of thanks" is the proper speech for a Christian minister (Eph. 5:4). James declared, "If any man among you seem to be religious, and bridleth not his tongue, but deceiveth his own heart, this man's religion is vain" (Jas. 1:26).

Personality

Character is closely related to our values, those things we build a life on. Personality has more to do with attitude and relationship. Our character will determine what we try to get done, and our personality will largely affect how well we get it done. Certain personality ingredients make us more effective in ministry.

A positive, optimistic, joyful, confident person, for example, is more effective than one who is negative, pessimistic, gloomy, and apprehensive. The Holy Spirit works in our lives to bring forth those positive characteristics; the fruit of the Spirit includes love, joy, and peace. Paul in his ministry displayed these qualities even in the most difficult circumstances. From prison he wrote, "Rejoice in the Lord alway: and again I say, Rejoice" (Phil. 4:4).

Enthusiastic and energetic persons are generally more successful in ministry than those who are apathetic and indifferent. Enthusiasm and energy combined with discipline, planning, and hard, effective work are a dynamic combination for ministry.

Generous, hospitable, trusting ministers are more useful in God's service than those who are greedy, selfish, and suspicious. Generosity normally grows out of a spirit of contentment, of being at peace with oneself and God, of not being anxious about tomorrow or unsatisfied about current possessions, position, or honors. A person who is content is not likely to be envious, greedy, or jealous.

God wants us to have adequate material provision, but he does not want us to ruin our lives by an inordinate concern for position and possession. The New Testament indicates that a bishop should not be a lover of money (1 Tim. 3:3) and a deacon should not be greedy for gain (1 Tim. 3:8). Paul warned, "They that will be rich fall into temptation and a snare, and into many foolish and hurtful lusts, which drown men in destruction and perdition" (1 Tim. 6:9). And the writer of Hebrews warned, "Keep your lives free from the love of money and be content with what you have, because God has said, 'Never will I leave you; never will I forsake you'" (Heb. 13:5, NIV). James blamed killing and war on lust for position and possession: "You lust and do not have; so you commit murder. And you are envious and cannot obtain; so you fight and quarrel" (Jas. 4:1-2, NASB). The New Testament links covetousness with idolatry and lists greed along with adultery and thievery. Jesus declared war on materialism: "You cannot serve both God and money" (Luke 16:13b, NIV). He commanded his followers, "Do not lay up for yourselves treasures upon earth, where moth and rust destroy, and where thieves break in and steal. But lay up for yourselves treasures in heaven" (Matt. 6:19-20, NASB).

Sensitive, sympathetic, compassionate, gentle, caring—these adjectives also should describe the minister. In a sense, these are all dimensions of Christian love. As Paul wrote to the Ephesians, "And be ye kind one to another, tenderhearted, forgiving one another, even as God for Christ's sake hath forgiven you. Be ye therefore followers of God, as dear children; And walk in love, as Christ also hath loved us, and hath given himself for us an offering and sacrifice to God for a sweet-smelling savor" (Eph. 4:32 to 5:2).

Only the Lord Jesus himself was a totally fit instrument for ministry. The Scriptures say of him, "And being made perfect, he became the author of eternal salvation" (Heb. 5:9). No one else is perfect, not even a minister the caliber of Paul. To see all of these qualities of life, attributes of character, and traits of personality laid out could cause discouragement. But it shouldn't. These are like the lines on a road map—they indicate possibilities on a pilgrimage, not demands for immediate accomplishment. The Bible sets these forth for encouragement, not discouragement. They are the goals toward which God helps us move. As we embody more and more of them, we will become more and more effective in ministry, increasingly fit instruments in God's hand for powerful service to others.

And Finally

The setting was a restaurant atop a skyscraper overlooking one of American's largest cities. The participants, in addition to myself, were two attorneys, partners in a prestigious firm, each recognized as an outstanding expert in his field. The occasion was partly celebration—the firm had just won a big lawsuit—and partly deliberation—the firm was at a crossroads concerning its future development.

As the evening progressed, these two brilliant Christians discussed more than business. They talked about life, its purpose and meaning. They agreed that life should be more than making money, succeeding in a profession, or collecting things. Life, they said, should major on ministering to and helping others; it is summed up in service, meeting human need out of Christian love.

People such as my two friends are the inspiration of this book as well as its object. Clearly God has saved us in order to send us on the mission of service. We are to be ready to minister. Although our ministries will vary greatly, they all have a common purpose—out of love to meet the needs of others to the glory of God. This is our vocation. This is our life.